10 Minute Guide to Norton Desktop™ for Windows™

Michael L. Miller

a
alpha books

A Division of Prentice Hall Computer Publishing

11711 North College, Carmel, Indiana 46032 USA

International Standard Book Number: 1-56761-025-0
Library of Congress Catalog Card Number: 92-82730

95 94 93 92 8 7 6 5 4 3 2 1

Interpretation of the printing code: the rightmost number of the first series of numbers is the year of the book's printing; the rightmost number of the second series of numbers is the number of the book's printing. For example, a printing code of 92-1 shows that the first printing of the book occurred in 1992.

Publisher: *Marie Butler-Knight*
Managing Editor: *Elizabeth Keaffaber*
Acquisitions Editor: *Steve Poland*
Development Editor: *Faithe Wempen*
Production Editor: *Annalise N. DiPaolo*
Copy Editors: *Audra Gable and Howard Peirce*
Cover Designer: *Dan Armstrong*
Designer: *Michele Laseau*
Indexers: *John Sleeva*
Production Team: *Scott Boucher, Lisa Daugherty, Dennis Clay Hager, John Kane, Bob LaRoche, Roger Morgan, Angela Pozdol, Susan Shepard, Angie Trzepacz, Lisa Wilson, Alyssa Yesh*

Special thanks to Hilary Adams for assuring the technical accuracy of this book.

Screen reproductions in this book were created by means of the program Collage Plus from Inner Media, Inc., Hollis, NH.

Printed in the United States of America

Contents

Introduction

You've just installed Norton Desktop for Windows on your PC. You're staring at the multiple volumes of documentation, wondering just how you're going to get started with this new program. Now what?

A few things are certain:

- You need a method of finding your way around the Norton Desktop quickly and easily.
- You need to identify and learn the tasks necessary to accomplish your particular goals.
- You need a clear-cut, plain-English guide to the basic features of the program.

Welcome to the *10 Minute Guide to Norton Desktop for Windows*

Because you don't have the luxury of sitting down uninterrupted for hours at a time to learn Norton Desktop for Windows, this *10 Minute Guide* presents lessons that can be completed in 10 minutes or less. Since you are presented information in bite-sized, self-contained modules, you can stop and start as often as you like. Now you can learn exactly what you need, at your own pace—and in 10 minutes or less!

What is the *10 Minute Guide*?

The *10 Minute Guide* is a new approach to learning computer programs. Instead of trying to teach you everything about a particular software product (and ending up with a 1000-page book in the process), the *10 Minute Guide* teaches you only the most often-used features, using a series of short, focused lessons.

The *10 Minute Guide* teaches you about programs without relying on technical jargon. With straightforward, easy-to-follow explanations and special artwork, called *icons*, to call your attention to important tips and definitions, the *10 Minute Guide* makes learning a new software program fun and easy.

The following icons help you find your way around in the *10 Minute Guide to Norton Desktop for Windows:*

Plain English These definitions appear wherever a new term is introduced.

Timesaver Tips These tips offer you shortcuts and hints for using the program efficiently and effectively.

Panic Button These identify areas where new users might run into trouble, and offer practical solutions to potential problems.

Specific conventions are used to help you find your way around the Norton Desktop as easily as possible:

`On-screen text`	On-screen text will appear in a special monospace font.
`What you type`	Information you type will appear in a bold, color, monospace font.
Items you select	Items you select or keys you press will appear in color.
Selection keys	Boldface letters within a menu, command, or option name indicate selection keys for keyboard shortcuts. These correspond to the underlined letters on-screen.

In addition, this book assumes that you are familiar with Windows and Windows operating conventions. It is assumed that you will be using Norton Desktop with a mouse, although many instructions can also be implemented with the keyboard. If you are not familiar with Windows operations, refer to the DOS and Windows Primer at the back of this book.

The *10 Minute Guide to Norton Desktop for Windows* is organized into 27 lessons, ranging from general operation to specific utilities. Remember, however, that nothing in this book is difficult. All lessons can be completed in 10 minutes or less.

Who Should Use the *10 Minute Guide to Norton Desktop for Windows?*

The *10 Minute Guide to Norton Desktop for Windows* is for anyone who:

- Needs to learn Norton Desktop quickly.
- Wants a clear, concise guide to the most important features of the Norton Desktop.
- Is adding Norton Desktop to their Windows environment and needs a quick guide to the essential program features.

What Is Norton Desktop for Windows?

Norton Desktop for Windows combines an operating environment that runs "on top of" regular Windows with user tools and utility programs. (This means you must have Windows to run Norton Desktop for Windows.)

Norton Desktop for Windows is, first and foremost, a "shell" program that replaces the normal Windows Program Manager shell. It uses a combination of menus and icons to provide an easy-to-use, flexible operating environment.

Norton Desktop for Windows is also a collection of user tools and utilities. These "miniprograms" enable you to perform a variety of useful tasks, including backing up your hard disk and changing the appearance of your desktop icons.

For Further Reference . . .

Alpha Books publishes several other books that will help increase your productivity in the Windows environment after you've completed this *10 Minute Guide*:

The 10 Minute Guide to Windows 3.1, by Kate Barnes.

The First Book of Windows 3.1, Bestseller Edition, by Jack Nimersheim

Trademarks

All terms mentioned in this book that are known to be trademarks or service marks are listed here. In addition, terms suspected of being trademarks or service marks have been appropriately capitalized. Alpha Books cannot attest to the accuracy of this information. Use of a term in this book should not be regarded as affecting the validity of any trademark or service mark.

Norton Desktop is a trademark of SYMANTEC.
Windows is a trademark of Microsoft Corporation.

For Further Reference . . .

Alpha Books publishes several other books that will help increase your productivity in the Windows environment after you've completed this *10 Minute Guide*:

> *The 10 Minute Guide to Windows 3.1*, by Kate Barnes.
>
> *The First Book of Windows 3.1, Bestseller Edition*, by Jack Nimersheim

Trademarks

All terms mentioned in this book that are known to be trademarks or service marks are listed here. In addition, terms suspected of being trademarks or service marks have been appropriately capitalized. Alpha Books cannot attest to the accuracy of this information. Use of a term in this book should not be regarded as affecting the validity of any trademark or service mark.

Norton Desktop is a trademark of SYMANTEC.
Windows is a trademark of Microsoft Corporation.

Lessons

Lesson 1

Starting and Exiting Norton Desktop for Windows

In this lesson, you'll learn how to start and end a typical Norton Desktop session.

Starting Norton Desktop for Windows

When you installed Norton Desktop for Windows, you were asked if you wanted the Norton Desktop to replace Program Manager as your Windows shell. If you answered *yes* (the default), Norton Desktop automatically starts when you start Windows.

Shell A *shell* is a simple interface that surrounds a more complex program. The standard shell for Windows is called the Program Manager; the Norton Desktop provides an easier-to-use shell that can be used in place of the Program Manager.

To start Windows and Norton Desktop together, follow these steps:

1. From the DOS prompt, type **WIN** and press Enter.

2. The Windows start-up screen appears while Windows and Norton Desktop are loading.

3. The Norton Desktop appears on-screen (see Figure 1.1).

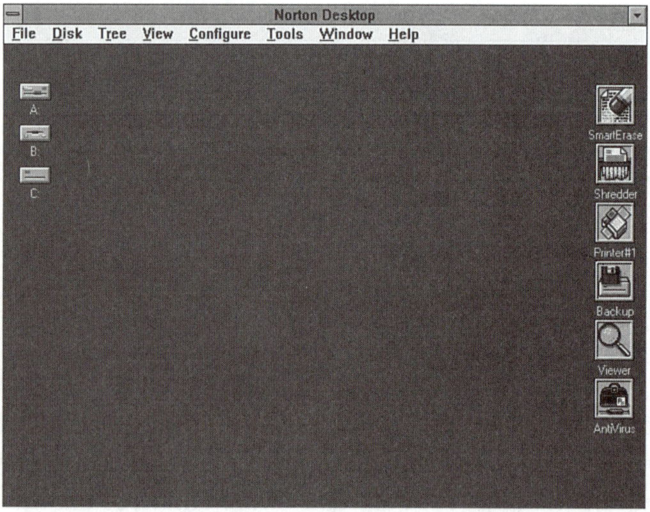

Figure 1.1 The Norton Desktop.

Where Is It? If the Norton Desktop does not appear when you start Windows, you need to edit one of the Windows start-up files. Using a text editor (such as the DOS 5 Editor), open the SYSTEM.INI file and locate the line that reads `SHELL=PROGMAN.EXE`. Edit this line so that it reads `SHELL=NDW.EXE`. When you save the SYSTEM.INI file and restart Windows, Norton Desktop will now be your Windows shell.

All Norton Desktop operations are performed from the menu bar or from individual desktop icons. You'll learn more about the menus and icons in later lessons, as well as the specific operations.

•

Exiting Norton Desktop for Windows

There are two ways to exit Windows and the Norton Desktop and return to DOS.

1. Double-click the Control menu button in the upper left corner of the screen (see Figure 1.2).
2. When the dialog box asks if you wish to exit, answer Yes.

Or

1. Pull down the File menu.
2. Select the Exit option (see Figure 1.2).
3. When the dialog box asks if you wish to exit, answer Yes.

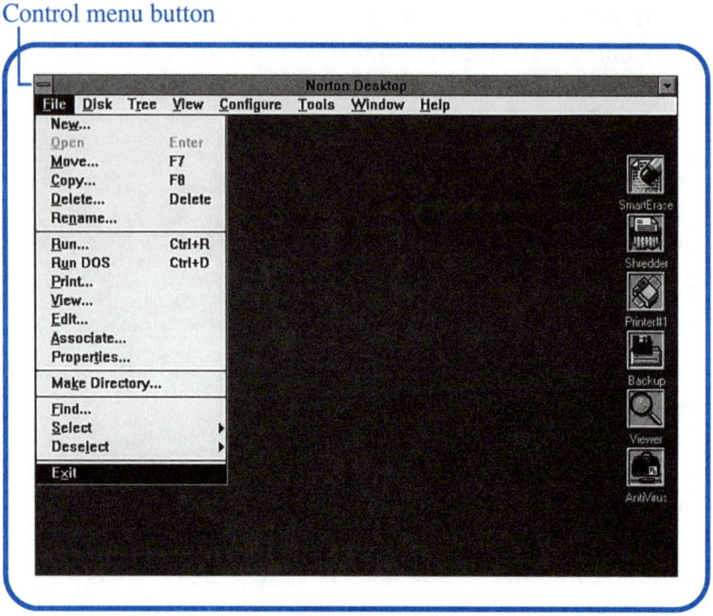

Figure 1.2 Exiting Norton Desktop.

In this lesson, you learned how to enter and exit the Norton Desktop. In the next lesson, you will learn how to navigate around the parts of the Norton Desktop.

Lesson 2

Navigating the Norton Desktop

In this lesson, you'll learn the parts of the Norton Desktop and how to move around on the Desktop using the mouse and keyboard.

Introducing the Norton Desktop

Just as the top of your desk holds all the tools you use to work in your office, the Norton Desktop "holds" all the software and utilities installed on your computer system. It supplements the normal Microsoft Windows environment with a series of *icons* and *pull-down menus* that perform specific operations.

Icons An *icon* is a small picture that represents a software program or utility. Select a Norton Desktop icon to open the corresponding program.

While the Norton Desktop can be minimized like any other Windows application, it is normally maximized to fill the entire screen. The Norton Desktop (see Figure 2.1) includes the following elements:

Title bar Displays the title of the active program, in this case Norton Desktop.

Control menu button Click here to pull down the Norton Desktop Control menu.

Menu bar Displays individual Norton Desktop menus; each menu pulls down to display additional menu items.

Minimize button Click here to shrink the Norton Desktop to an icon.

Drive icons Represent individual drives on your computer system; double-click on these icons to display drive windows.

Tool icons Represent Norton Desktop's main user tools; double-click on these icons to activate the tools.

Application icons Represent currently running applications or program groups in a minimized state; double-click on these icons to maximize the applications or open the program groups.

Desktop icons Represent applications, documents, and utilities; double-click on these icons to launch the applications.

Later lessons will show you how to use these elements to perform specific tasks.

Lesson 2

Navigating the Norton Desktop

In this lesson, you'll learn the parts of the Norton Desktop and how to move around on the Desktop using the mouse and keyboard.

Introducing the Norton Desktop

Just as the top of your desk holds all the tools you use to work in your office, the Norton Desktop "holds" all the software and utilities installed on your computer system. It supplements the normal Microsoft Windows environment with a series of *icons* and *pull-down menus* that perform specific operations.

Icons An *icon* is a small picture that represents a software program or utility. Select a Norton Desktop icon to open the corresponding program.

While the Norton Desktop can be minimized like any other Windows application, it is normally maximized to fill the entire screen. The Norton Desktop (see Figure 2.1) includes the following elements:

Title bar Displays the title of the active program, in this case Norton Desktop.

Control menu button Click here to pull down the Norton Desktop Control menu.

Menu bar Displays individual Norton Desktop menus; each menu pulls down to display additional menu items.

Minimize button Click here to shrink the Norton Desktop to an icon.

Drive icons Represent individual drives on your computer system; double-click on these icons to display drive windows.

Tool icons Represent Norton Desktop's main user tools; double-click on these icons to activate the tools.

Application icons Represent currently running applications or program groups in a minimized state; double-click on these icons to maximize the applications or open the program groups.

Desktop icons Represent applications, documents, and utilities; double-click on these icons to launch the applications.

Later lessons will show you how to use these elements to perform specific tasks.

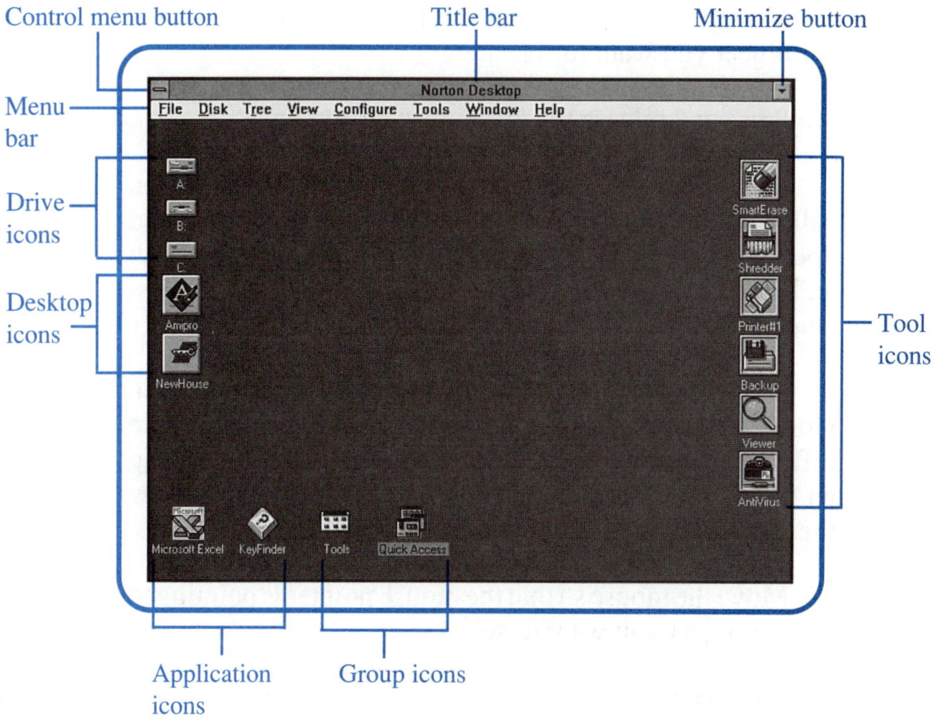

Figure 2.1 The elements of the Norton Desktop.

Moving with the Mouse

Norton Desktop, like Windows, was designed to be used with a mouse. The two most important mouse operations to master are *pointing and clicking* and *dragging and dropping*. Both of these operations are essential for efficient use of Norton Desktop.

Pointing and clicking is a simple operation. It's most often used to select icons, open pull-down menus, or select commands. Follow these steps:

1. Move the mouse so that the mouse pointer is on the object you want to select.

2. Press and release the left mouse button once.

Many operations involve a variation of this operation called *double-clicking*, often used to launch programs and open program groups. To double-click, point at an object and then click the left mouse button twice in rapid succession.

Dragging and dropping, used to copy and move files in Norton Desktop drive windows, is only slightly more difficult. You can practice this by dragging and dropping an icon on the desktop. (It won't hurt anything.) Follow these steps:

1. Move the mouse so that the mouse pointer is pointing to the object you want to select.

2. Press and hold down the left mouse button.

3. Move the mouse without releasing the mouse button, and drag the object to a new location.

4. When the object is in place, release the mouse button.

Using the Keyboard

Norton Desktop was designed to be used with a mouse, but there are some operations that may be more convenient to do from the keyboard.

Key Combinations When you see two key names joined by a plus sign (+), press and hold down the first key, press the second key, and release both keys. For example, when you see Ctrl+End, hold down the Ctrl key and press the End key.

While desktop icons cannot be accessed via the keyboard, you can use the keyboard to access commands on Norton Desktop menus. Follow these steps:

1. Press Alt. This activates the menu bar (see Figure 2.2).
2. Use → and ← to move to the menu of your choice.
3. Press ↓ to pull down the menu.
4. Use ↑ and ↓ to move to the menu option of your choice.
5. Press Enter to select the menu option, or press Esc to close the menu without selecting an option.

Figure 2.2 The File menu highlighted in the menu bar.

Selecting Items Quickly To access any on-screen underlined item, press Alt plus the underlined letter. In this book, letters which are underlined on-screen are boldfaced. For example, you can select **F**ile **S**ave by pressing Alt, F, S.

In this lesson, you learned the parts of the Norton Desktop and how to use the mouse and keyboard to operate the Desktop. In the next lesson, you will learn more about Norton Desktop's menus.

Lesson 3

Using Norton Desktop Menus

In this lesson, you'll learn how to use Norton Desktop's menu system.

Most Norton Desktop commands can be invoked from the menu system. The main menu bar contains pull-down menus which you use to access various submenus. From these submenus, you can initiate a variety of Norton Desktop operations.

Norton Desktop's Main Menu Bar

Norton Desktop's main menu bar contains eight menus (see Figure 3.1), each with numerous options and submenus:

File Manipulates and configures files; operations include **O**pen, **C**opy, **D**elete, and **V**iew.

Disk Manipulates disks and network drives; operations include Copy Diskette and Format Diskette.

Tree Lets you expand and contract the directory trees displayed in Norton Desktop's drive windows.

View Provides viewing options for drive windows and the Norton Viewer.

Configure Lets you configure and customize the Norton Desktop and its tools.

Tools Provides direct access to Norton Desktop's tools and utilities.

Window Chooses various window views and provides direct access to individual program groups.

Help Provides access to the Norton Desktop Help system.

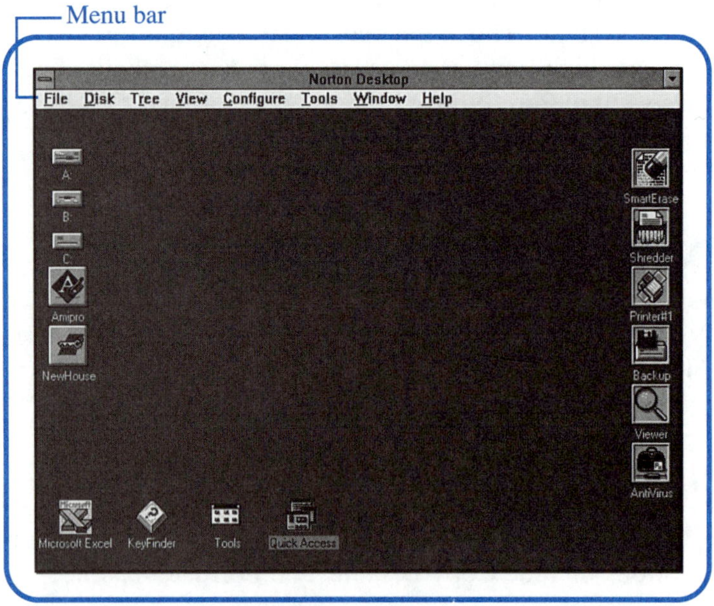

Figure 3.1 Norton Desktop's main menu bar.

Long Menus and Short Menus Norton Desktop gives you the choice of displaying either *long* or *short menus*. If you select short menus, you cannot access all the options available or discussed in this book. To display full menus, pull down the Configure menu, select the Load Menu command, and choose the FULL option from the Load Menu dialog box.

Using the Menu System

Follow these steps to select an item from one of the main menus:

1. Move the mouse pointer to desired menu.
2. Click the left mouse button to pull down the menu (see Figure 3.2).
3. Move the mouse pointer to the desired menu option.
4. Click the left mouse button to activate the menu option.

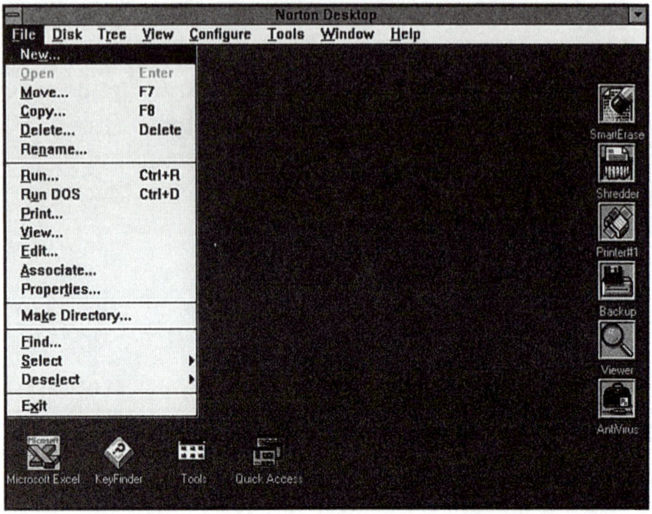

Figure 3.2 The menu bar with the **F**ile menu pulled down.

In this lesson, you learned about Norton Desktop's menu system. In the next lesson you will learn how to use Norton Desktop's various icons.

Lesson 4

Using Norton Desktop Icons

In this lesson, you'll learn how to use the various types of icons that are part of the Norton Desktop.

Norton Desktop makes extensive use of *icons*, small pictures that represent larger objects. Norton Desktop lets you use icons for various operations, including launching programs.

The Different Types of Icons in Norton Desktop

Icons in Norton Desktop can represent a wide variety of objects, including:

Applications Programs you can run from the desktop.

Documents Text files you can edit or view.

Drive windows A visual representation of all the files or a selected drive.

Quick Access groups Groups of files or programs.

Group items Anything in a Quick Access group.

Norton Desktop tools The main software tools that are included with Norton Desktop.

Figure 4.1 shows examples of some of these types of icons.

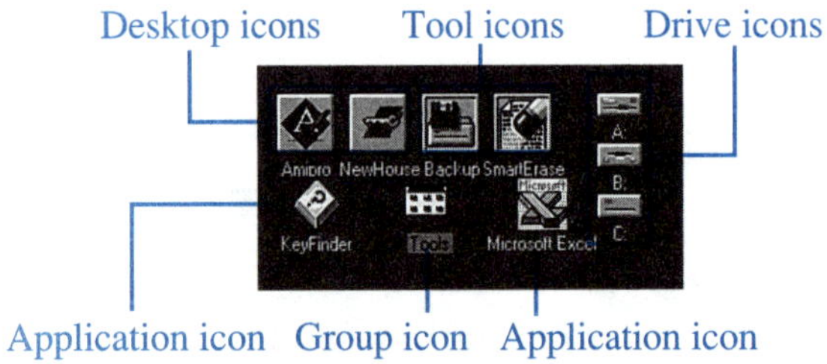

Figure 4.1 Various types of Norton Desktop icons.

Putting Icons to Use

You use the mouse to activate icons. Depending on the type of icon, activating an icon can maximize a minimized application or document, launch a new application or document, or open a group or drive window.

To activate an icon, follow these steps:

1. Move the mouse pointer to the desired icon.
2. Double-click the left mouse button.

You also use the mouse to *move* icons. (Remember the drag-and-drop procedure from Lesson 2?) Follow these steps:

1. Move the mouse pointer to the desired icon.

2. Press and hold down the left mouse button.

3. Move the mouse without releasing the mouse button, and drag the icon to a new location.

4. When the icon is in place, release the mouse button.

Moving Icons between Program Groups In addition to moving icons around the Desktop, you can also use drag and drop to move icons from one Quick Access group to another. You'll learn more about Quick Access groups in Lesson 5.

Creating New Desktop Icons

You can create new Desktop icons by dragging existing icons from group windows or files from drive windows. Follow these steps:

1. Open the desired group window or drive window.

2. Select the desired icon or file with the mouse.

3. Press and hold down the left mouse button.

4. Move the mouse without releasing the mouse button, and drag the icon from the current window to the Desktop (see Figure 4.2).

5. When the icon is in place, release the mouse button.

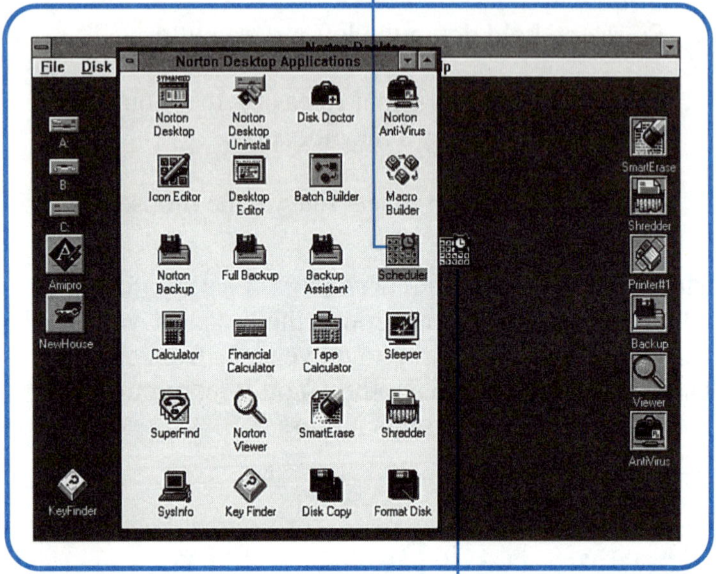

Figure 4.2 Dragging an icon from a group window and dropping it onto the Desktop.

In this lesson, you learned how to use and create Norton Desktop icons. In the next lesson you learn how to use Norton Desktop's Quick Access groups.

Lesson 5

Using Quick Access Groups

In this lesson, you learn how to use and manage Norton Desktop's Quick Access groups.

A *group* in Norton Desktop is a collection of icons contained in a window. Each icon in a group can represent either an individual application or another group. These groups are part of Norton Desktop's *Quick Access* system, and are called *Quick Access Groups (QAGs)*. Mastering Quick Access groups is key to mastering Norton Desktop.

Activating Quick Access Groups

All groups are displayed as icons in the Quick Access window. To display the Quick Access window, double-click the *right* mouse button on any empty space on the Desktop.

Quick Access Window All of the individual Quick Access Groups (QAGs) appear as icons in the *Quick Access window*. This Quick Access window is like a "master group" that holds all the other groups.

Norton Desktop's QAGs work in much the same way as standard Windows program groups. Double-click the *left* mouse button on any icon to open the associated program or group.

Displaying Quick Access Groups

Like the program groups in Windows, QAGs can be minimized to an icon, opened as a window, or maximized to fill the entire screen.

Program Groups versus QAGs With Windows program groups, minimizing one (with the minimize arrow) and closing it (with the control menu) accomplish the same thing. It's different with QAGs. Minimizing a QAG places it as an icon on the desktop, while closing a QAG returns it to the Quick Access window.

Open QAGs can be displayed in one of three different styles (shown in Figure 5.1): icon style, list style, and toolbox style. Icon style is the default.

To change the display style for any Quick Access group, follow these steps:

1. Open the desired QAG.
2. Pull down the Window menu and select View Group As. The View Group As dialog box appears (Figure 5.2).
3. Open the drop-down list of choices for View Group As.

4. Select the desired view option.

5. Choose OK. The QAG is now displayed in the format you specified.

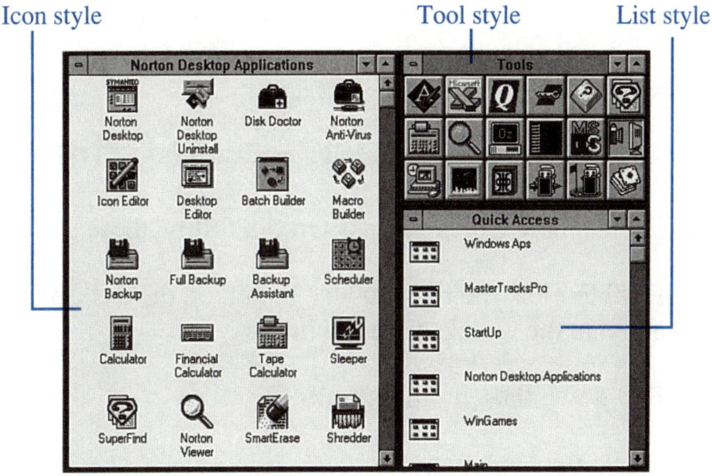

Figure 5.1 Quick Access groups displayed in icon, list, and toolbox styles.

Identical Icons The Toolbox view does not display any text—only icons, so this view is helpful only if every icon in that group looks different. In the Quick Access window, where all icons are identical, the Toolbox view would be useless!

Resizing Changed Group Windows You may need to resize a group window after you change display styles. One easy way to do so is by dragging its borders.

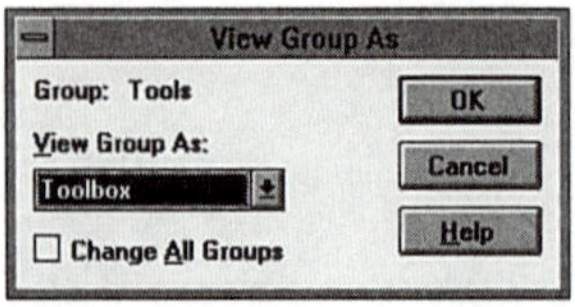

Figure 5.2 The View Group As dialog box.

Creating New Quick Access Groups

To create a new Quick Access Group, follow these steps:

1. Double-click the right mouse button on the desktop to activate the Quick Access window.
2. Pull down the File menu.
3. Select the New option.
4. When the New dialog box appears (see Figure 5.3), select Group and assign the group a Title (the label you assign to the group) and a Group File Name (the eight-character DOS filename).
5. If you wish to change the default icon, select the Icon option and select a new icon in the Choose Icon dialog box; select OK to close the dialog box.
6. Select OK to create the group.

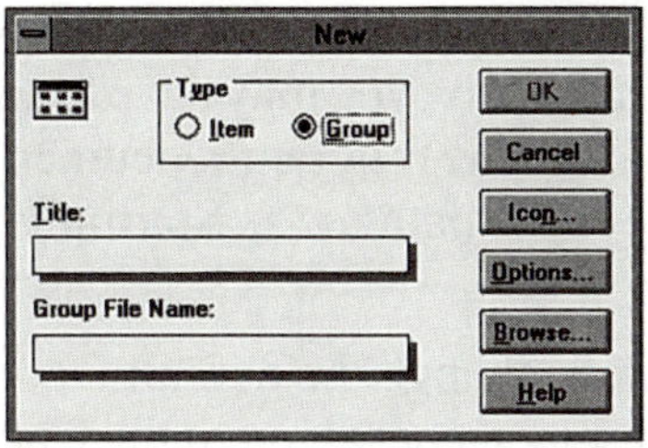

Figure 5.3 The New dialog box.

Adding Items to Quick Access Groups

There are two ways to add items to existing Quick Access Groups. You can use the menu system, or you can drag and drop icons from other groups.

To use the menu system to add a new item to a group, follow these steps:

1. Open the QAG where you want to add the new icon, and make sure that it's the active group.
2. Pull down the File menu.
3. Select the New option.
4. When the New dialog box appears, select the Item, and assign the item a Title.
5. In the Program/Document/Script box, enter the full path and file name of the associated program.

Your File Doesn't Launch If your file doesn't launch properly, you may have to select the Options option from the Program/Document/Script box and add the file's path to the Startup Directory box.

6. If you wish to change the default icon, select the Icon option and select a new icon in the Choose Icon dialog box; choose OK to close the dialog box.
7. Select OK to add the item.

Browsing for File Names If you can't remember the exact path and file name of an item to add, select the Browse button to display the Browse dialog box (see Figure 5.4). This dialog box lets you scroll through all the directories on your disk until you locate the file you need. Norton Desktop uses Browse dialog boxes throughout the program.

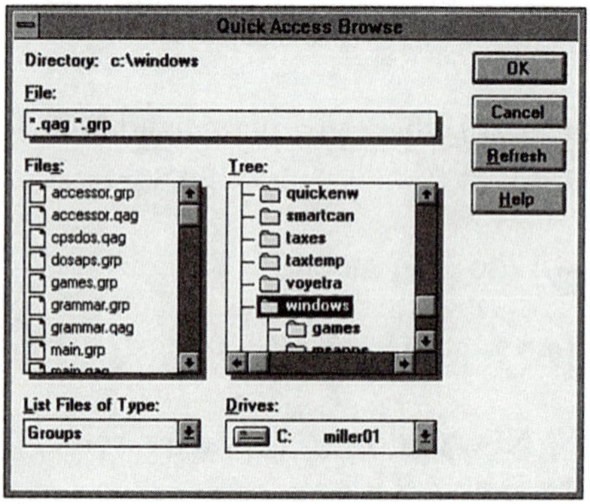

Figure 5.4 A Browse dialog box.

To add an item to a group using drag and drop, follow these steps:

1. Open both the source and the target Quick Access Groups.

2. Select the icon to move in the source group.

3. Click and hold the left mouse button and drag the icon from the source group.

4. Release the mouse button to drop it into the target group.

Deleting Group Items

To delete an icon from a Quick Access Group, follow these steps:

1. Select the icon.

2. Press the Del key or pull down the File menu and select Delete.

3. When Norton Desktop prompts you to confirm the deletion, select Yes.

Dangerous Deletions! Deleting QAGs is easy—*too* easy. Make sure that all the icons you need have been moved to a different QAG before you delete.

In this lesson, you learned how to use Norton Desktop's Quick Access Groups. In the next lesson, you will learn how to manipulate Norton Desktop's drive windows.

Lesson 6

Using Drive Windows

In this lesson, you learn how to use Norton Desktop's drive windows for drive, directory, and file management.

All data on your system is contained in *files*. Each file is part of a *directory*; directories may include numerous nested *subdirectories*. All directories branch off of one main directory, called the *root directory*. Each drive on your system has its own root directory and *directory tree* of unique directories and files. The ability to manipulate drives, directories, and individual files is key to effective computer operation.

Understanding Drive Windows

Norton Desktop displays the contents of each drive in a unique *drive window*. The drive window visually represents each drive's directory tree and files. You use drive windows to copy, move, rename, and delete files and directories, as explained in later lessons.

A Norton Desktop drive window (see Figure 6.1) includes the following elements:

Drive selector Displays the current drive and label and lets you select other drives.

Drive status box Displays the unused disk space on the current drive.

Directory/file status box Displays information about the current directory and/or selected files.

Tree pane Displays the directory tree for the current drive.

File pane Displays the files in the current directory.

Button bar Contains buttons that let you directly access common file operations.

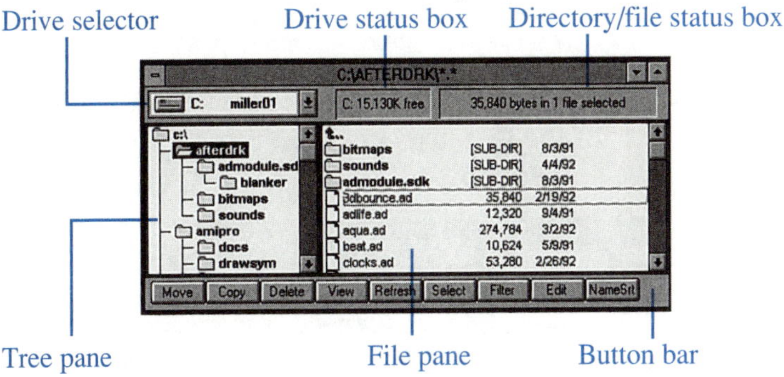

Figure 6.1 The elements of a drive window.

Opening Drive Windows

Drive windows are shown as icons on the Norton Desktop. All active drives on your system are represented by icons, including hard disk and floppy disk drives. You open the desired drive window by double-clicking on the appropriate icon.

You can also open a drive window using the menu system. Follow these steps:

1. Pull down the Windows menu.
2. Select the Open Drive Window option.
3. When the Open Drive dialog box appears, select the drive from the drop-down list box.
4. Select OK to open the drive window.

Opening the View Pane

In addition to the standard directory and file panes, the drive window can also display a *view pane*. This pane lets you see the contents of the selected file (see Figure 6.2).

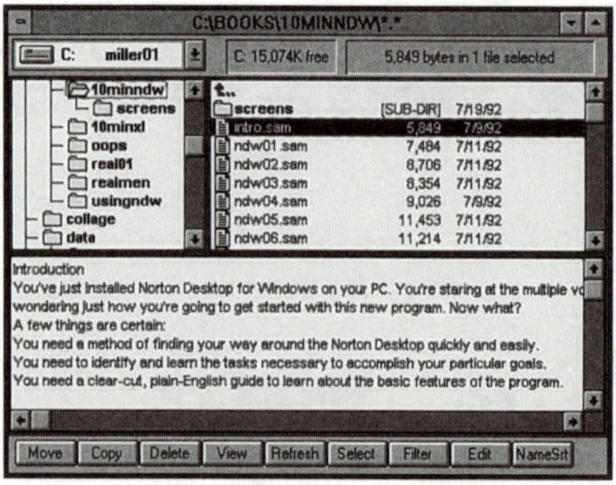

Figure 6.2 A drive window with the view pane activated.

To activate the view pane, follow these steps:

1. Open the desired drive window.

2. Click the View button on the button bar.

Removing the View Pane The View button works like an on/off switch. Click the View button a second time to remove the view pane from the drive window.

Displaying All Files on Your Drive

You can also display a list of all files on your drive, regardless of directory order. Follow these steps:

1. Open the desired drive window.

2. Pull down the View menu.

3. Select the Show Entire Drive option.

4. Select OK to display the file list.

Configuring Your File Listings

Norton Desktop allows you to display only certain types of files. For example, you can display only program files, or you can display all document files that have the archive attribute. Follow these steps:

1. Pull down the View menu.

2. Select the Filter command.

3. When the Filter dialog box appears (see Figure 6.3), select the desired types of files to display. (The default is **All** Files.)

4. Select OK to implement the changes.

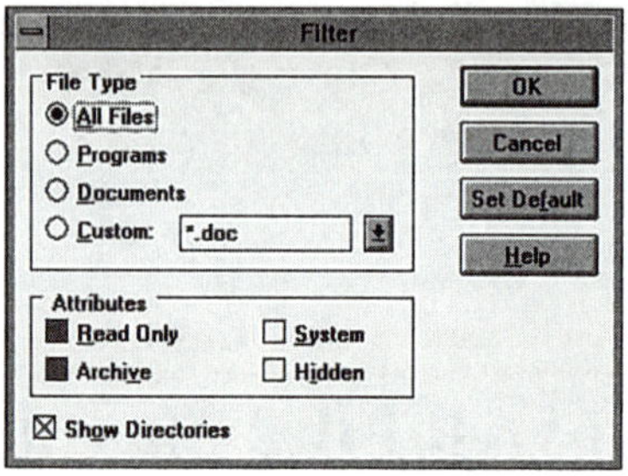

Figure 6.3 The Filter dialog box.

You can also display various details about each file, such as its attributes or the date and time it was last modified. Follow these steps:

1. Pull down the **V**iew menu.

2. Select the File **D**etails option.

3. When the File Details dialog box appears (see Figure 6.4), select the desired details you wish to display.

4. Select OK to implement the changes.

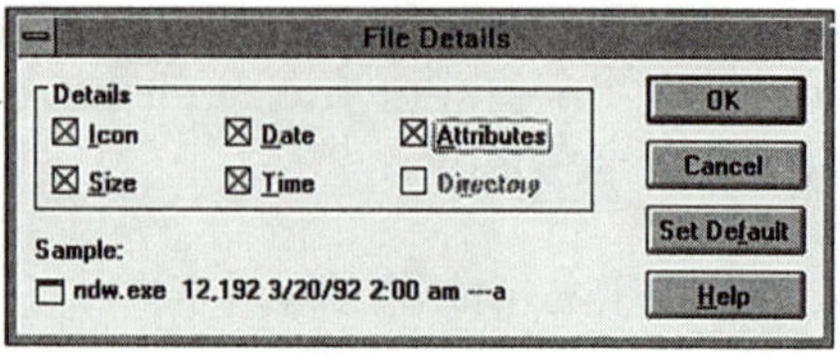

Figure 6.4 The File Details dialog box.

This lesson presented you with drive window basics. In the next lesson, you will learn how to work with diskettes.

Lesson 7

Formatting and Copying Diskettes

In this lesson, you learn to use Norton Desktop to format and copy diskettes, two essential tasks.

Formatting Diskettes

Diskettes must be *formatted* before you can use them. While some blank diskettes are sold preformatted, most are not. Fortunately, formatting diskettes with Norton Desktop is easy.

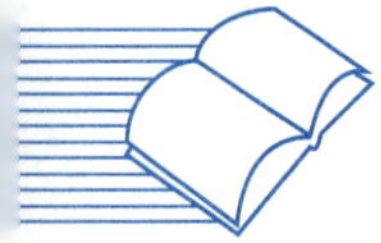

Formatting Disks must be prepared in a special format that the disk operating system can understand. During *formatting*, each disk is divided into tracks and sectors, so that the operating system can quickly locate specific data.

To format a diskette, follow these steps:

1. Pull down the Disk menu.
2. Select the Format Diskette command; the Format Diskette dialog box (see Figure 7.1) appears.

3. Select the diskette drive you are using.

4. Select the proper storage capacity of the diskette to be formatted.

5. Select Destructive in the **F**ormat Type box.

6. If you want to assign a label to the diskette, type a name in the **V**olume Label box.

7. Select OK to begin formatting.

8. When you are prompted to insert a blank diskette, do so.

9. When formatting is complete, you will be asked if you want to format another diskette. Answer Yes to repeat steps 3 through 8, or No to return to the Format Diskette dialog box.

10. Choose Cancel to close the dialog box.

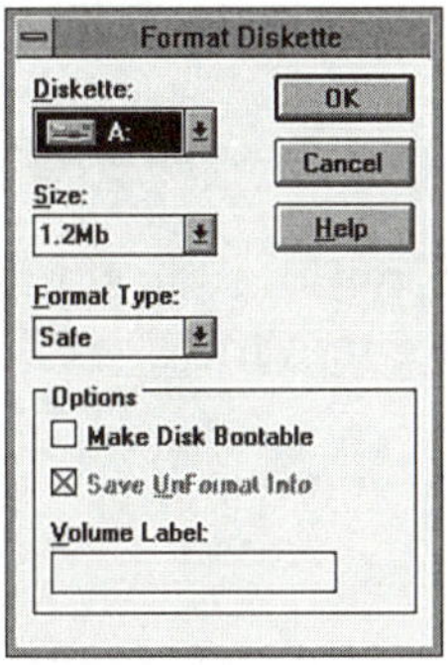

Figure 7.1 The Format Diskette dialog box.

Formatting Hard Disks You can format only diskettes with Norton Desktop; you cannot format hard disks.

Copying Entire Diskettes

In addition to copying individual files (discussed in Lesson 8), you can copy entire diskettes. To perform this operation, the source and the target diskettes must be of the exact same size and type. Follow these steps:

1. Pull down the Disk menu.
2. Select the Copy Diskette command; the Copy Diskette dialog box (see Figure 7.2) appears.
3. Select the source drive from the **F**rom box.
4. Select the target drive from the **T**o box.
5. Insert the original diskette in the drive.
6. Select OK to begin the copying process.
7. When prompted, remove the source diskette and insert the target diskette into the drive.
8. When prompted, remove the source diskette and reinsert the target diskette into the drive.
9. Repeat steps 7 and 8 as necessary.
10. After the copy operation is complete, you are asked if you want to make another copy. Choose No to end the copy operation.

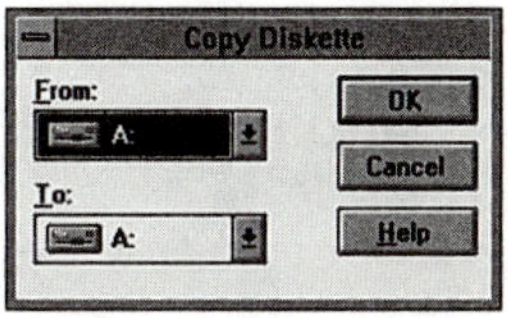

Figure 7.2 The Copy Diskette dialog box.

Wrong Size! You cannot copy diskettes of different sizes or types. For example, you cannot copy a 3 ½" diskette to a 5 ¼" diskette or a double-density diskette to a high-density diskette.

In this lesson, you learned how to format and copy diskettes. In the next lesson, you will learn how to use Norton Desktop to manage your files and directories.

Lesson 8

Copying and Moving Files and Directories

In this lesson, you learn how to use Norton Desktop's drive windows for file and directory management.

Working with files is one of the main things you do with your computer. Norton Desktop's drive windows make it easy to copy and move files and directories just by pointing and clicking with the mouse.

The key to copying files with Norton Desktop is to open two drive windows at the same time. This allows you to drag files from one drive window and drop them into a new location in the second drive window.

Copying Files

To copy a file from one location to another, follow these steps:

1. Open the first drive window. This will be your *source* window.

2. Open the second drive window. This will be your *target* window. If you're copying from one directory to another on the same drive, simply click on the same drive icon again to open a second window for that drive.

3. Move to the source window and scroll through the directory and file panes until you locate the file you wish to copy.

4. Select the file to be copied, click and hold down the left mouse button, and drag the file to the target window (see Figure 8.1).

5. Drag the file to the desired directory in the target window and release the mouse button.

6. Close both drive windows when you are finished.

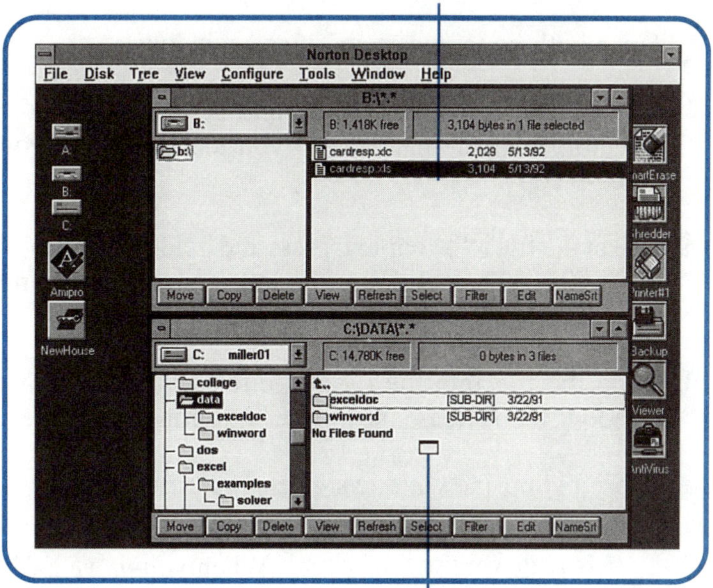

Figure 8.1 Dragging and dropping between two drive windows.

Copying Multiple Files You can drag and drop multiple files at one time. After you select the first file with the left mouse button, use the *right* mouse button to select additional files. When you drag the cursor from one window to another, all selected files will follow.

Moving Files

Moving files is similar to copying files, except that you hold down the Alt key while you drag the files. Follow these steps:

1. Open both your *source* and *target* windows.
2. Move to the source window and scroll through the directory and file panes until you locate the file you wish to copy.
3. Select the file to be copied, press and hold down the Alt key, click and hold down the left mouse button, and drag the file to the target window.
4. Drop the file into the desired directory in the target window, then release the mouse button and the Alt key.
5. Close both drive windows when you are finished.

Moving versus Copying When you *move* a file the original file is deleted from the target directory; when you *copy* a file the original file remains intact.

Copying Directories

Copying directories is similar to copying individual files. You select a directory in the directory pane (rather than a file in the file pane) and follow the steps presented for copying a file.

Calling All Subdirectories If you do not select all subdirectories within the desired directory, the subdirectories *will not* be copied. You must select the main directory and all its subdirectories for copying.

Moving Directories

As with copying directories, moving directories is similar to moving individual files. You select a directory in the directory pane and follow the steps outlined for moving a file.

In this lesson, you learned how to copy and move files and directories. In the next lesson, you learn how to rename and delete files and directories.

Lesson 9

Renaming and Deleting Files and Directories

In this lesson, you learn how to use Norton Desktop to rename and delete files and directories.

While Norton Desktop offers many ways to perform rename and delete operations, this book will focus on the easiest method: using the drive windows.

Renaming Files

To rename a file, follow these steps:

1. With the drive window open, select the file you wish to rename.
2. Pull down the File menu.
3. Select the Rename option.
4. When the Rename dialog appears (see Figure 9.1), type the new name in the **To** box.
5. Select OK to rename the file.

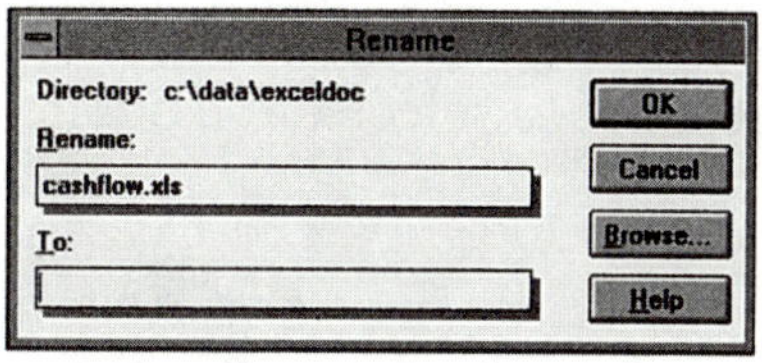

Figure 9.1 The Rename dialog box.

SuperVGA Renaming Shortcut If you use a SuperVGA display, you may see a Rename button on the drive window button bar. Click this button to display the Rename dialog box. (Regular VGA and EGA displays allow fewer buttons on the button bar than do higher-resolution displays.)

No Directory Name Change You can only change the name of a file; you cannot change the name of a directory.

Deleting Files and Directories

To delete a file or directory, follow these steps:

1. With the drive window open, select the file or directory you wish to delete.
2. Click the Delete button in the button bar or pull down the File menu and select the Delete option.
3. When asked to confirm the operation, select OK.

Shortcut Key Option You can also press the Del key to delete a selected file or directory.

Using SmartErase and Shredder to Delete Files You can use Norton Desktop's SmartErase utility to delete files. As described in Lesson 14, you simply drag a file from the drive window and drop it onto the SmartErase icon. You can also permanently shred your files by dropping them onto the Shredder icon, as described in Lesson 15.

In this lesson, you learned how to rename and delete files and directories. In the next lesson, you learn how to use Norton Desktop to print files without opening the associated software programs.

Lesson 10

Printing Files

In this lesson, you learn how to print files from the Norton Desktop.

Norton Desktop allows you to print document files without opening the associated program. For example, you can print Excel document files without opening Excel itself.

Associating Files

Before Norton Desktop can print a document file, it must know which software program is associated with the document file. This is called an *association.* Many common file types are automatically associated by Norton Desktop, but you may have to create associations for some types of files.

To associate a document file type with a particular program, follow these steps:

1. Pull down the File menu.

2. Select the Associate option; the Associate dialog box (shown in Figure 10.1) appears.

3. Type the file extension you wish to associate in the Extension box. For example, if you want to associate Excel .XLS files, type **XLS** in the box. (Do not include the period.)

4. Scroll through the list of program files and select the appropriate file to associate with.

5. Choose OK to complete the association.

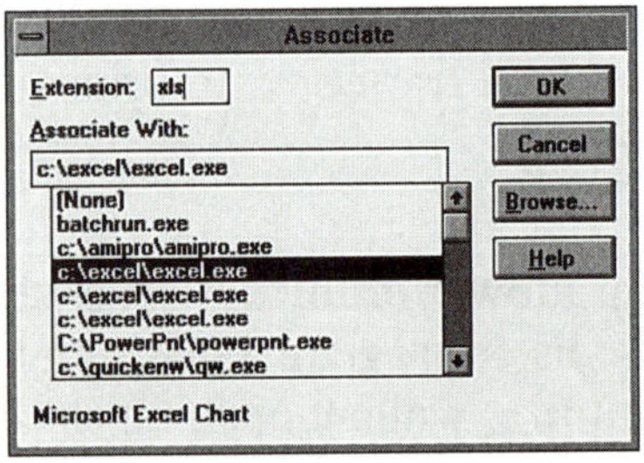

Figure 10.1 The Associate dialog box.

Printing from the Menu System

To print a file using the menu system, follow these steps:

1. Pull down the File menu.

2. Select the Print option; the Print dialog box (shown in Figure 10.2) appears.

3. Type the name of the file to print in the **Print** box.

4. Select the desired printer in the **To** box.

5. Choose OK to start printing.

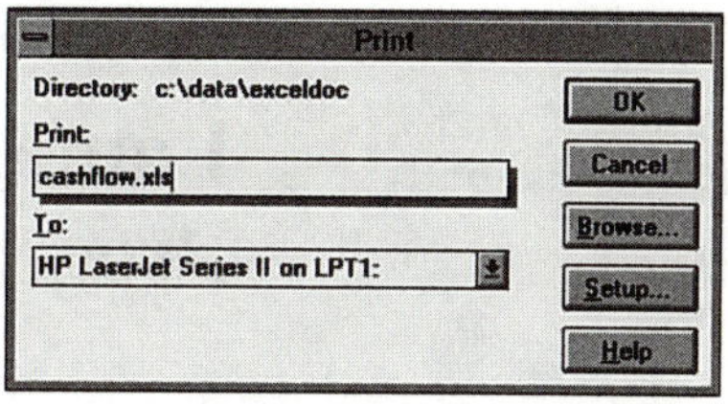

Figure 10.2 The Print dialog box.

When you select OK, Norton Desktop automatically launches the associated program and sends all the proper commands to start the printing process. After the file is printed, the associated program is automatically closed.

Printing Panic! When printing from the desktop, don't try to start a second print job before the first one is finished; the second job may not print properly. When printing from inside applications, multiple print jobs are okay.

Printing From the Drive Window

It's even easier to print from the drive window. Follow these steps:

1. With the drive window open, select the file to copy.
2. Drag the file from the drive window and drop it onto the Print icon.

In this lesson, you learned how to print files from the Norton Desktop. In the next lesson, you learn how to launch program files.

Lesson 11

Launching Program Files

In this lesson, you learn the various ways to launch program files from the Norton Desktop.

Norton Desktop is most frequently used to launch programs. There are many ways to launch programs with Norton Desktop; the most popular ones are presented here.

Launching Files from the Menu System

To launch a file using the menu system, follow these steps:

1. Pull down the File menu.
2. Select the Run option.
3. When the Run dialog box appears (as shown in Figure 11.1), type the exact path and file name of the program you wish to run.
4. Select OK to launch the program.

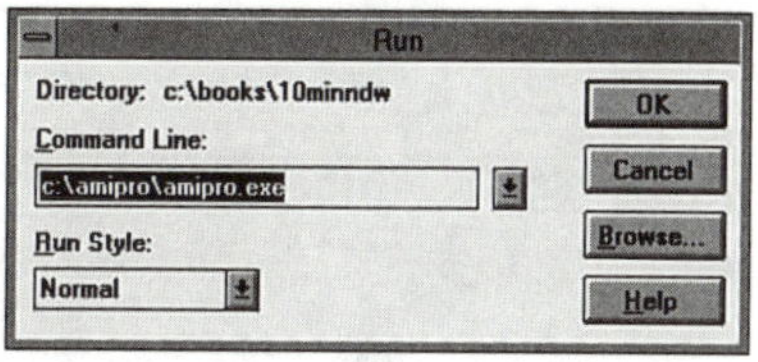

Figure 11.1 The Run dialog box.

Use Browse to Locate the File Remember, you can click on the Browse button to display the Browse dialog box to search for the file you wish to run.

Launching Files from the Launch List

Certain files are contained in the Launch List, accessed from the Control menu. To launch a file from the Launch List, follow these steps:

1. Click once on the button at the upper left corner of the Norton Desktop window to pull down the Control menu.

2. Select the Launch List option.

3. When the Launch List appears, as shown in Figure 11.2, select the file you wish to launch.

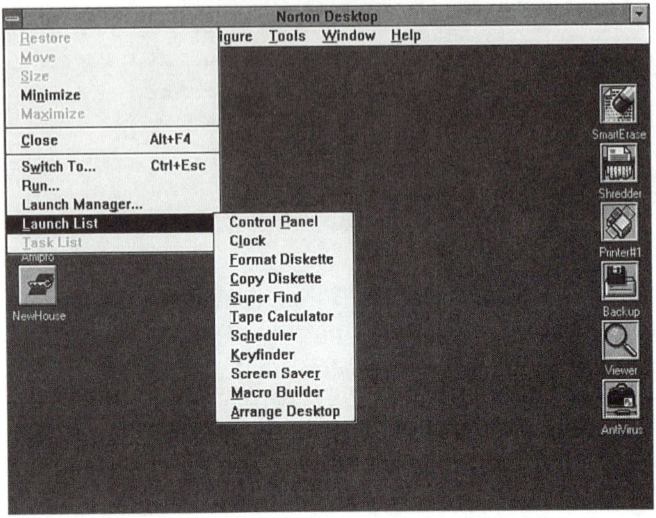

Figure 11.2 The Control menu Launch List.

To add a file to the launch list, follow these steps:

1. Pull down the Control menu.
2. Select the Launch Manager option.
3. When the Launch Manager dialog box appears, click on the Add button.
4. When the Add Launch List Item dialog box appears, type the label text for the program in the **T**ext box, the path and program name in the **C**ommand Line box, and the shortcut key (if desired) in the **S**hortcut Key box.
5. Select OK to confirm your selections.

Launching Files from the Drive Windows

To launch a file from a drive window, follow these steps:

1. With the drive window open, highlight the desired file name.

2. Double-click the left mouse button to launch the file.

Launching Document Files You can launch a program with a specific document loaded. From an open drive window, drag the document file and drop it onto the program file name or icon. The program will launch with the selected file opened. You can also double-click on the document file to achieve the same effect if the document is associated with the program file.

Launching Files from Desktop Icons

Launching files from desktop icons is perhaps the easiest way to launch your programs. Simply double-click on any desktop icon that represents a program and the program automatically launches.

Launching Files from Quick Access Groups

Launching a file from a Quick Access Group is the same as launching a file from a desktop icon. With the group open, double-click on the desired icon and the associated program automatically launches.

Automatically Launching Programs When You Start Norton Desktop You can specify certain files to launch automatically whenever you start Windows and Norton Desktop. Simply open the AutoStart or StartUp group, and drag the icon for the desired program into the open group window. The next time you start Norton Desktop for Windows, all programs in this group will launch automatically.

In this lesson, you learned several ways to launch your favorite programs with Norton Desktop. In the next lesson, you learn how to use Norton Backup to create backup copies of your valuable data.

Lesson 12

Backing Up Files with Norton Backup for Windows

In this lesson, you learn how to create backup copies of your valuable data with Norton Backup for Windows.

Your data is valuable; you need to protect it in case of an accident. The best protection comes in the form of backup copies made from your hard disk to a set of diskettes. If you do experience a loss of data, you can restore any lost or damaged files from your backup diskettes.

Norton Backup for Windows is a utility included with Norton Desktop that makes it easy for you to back up all or part of your hard disk. You should use Norton Backup on a regular basis to protect yourself from the effects of accidental data loss.

Backups Backing up data is different from copying data. A *backup copy* is created in a special file format that takes up less disk space than normal files, and is thus unreadable by your regular programs. A *backup set*, then, takes up fewer diskettes than if you simply copied your hard disk data to floppy diskettes.

Starting Norton Backup for Windows

If the Norton Backup icon appears on your desktop, double-click on the icon to launch the program. Otherwise, follow these steps to launch the program:

1. Pull down the Tools menu.
2. Select the Norton Backup option (to display the main Norton Backup window, shown in Figure 12.1).

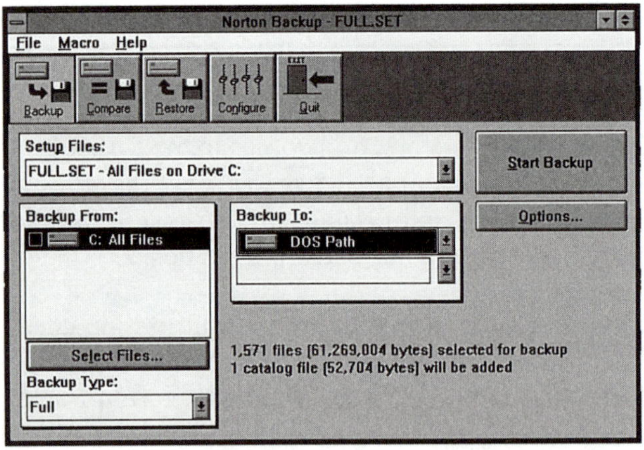

Figure 12.1 The main Norton Backup window.

Configuring Norton Backup for Windows

When you first launch Norton Backup, it automatically configures itself for your particular system. As the configuration begins, follow these steps:

1. From the Configure window (shown in Figure 12.2) select the drive you'll use for backups.

2. Select Start. A warning dialog box appears. Select OK to begin the testing.

3. When you are prompted to insert blank diskettes, do so.

4. When the testing is complete, Norton Backup compares the test backup data with the original data on your hard disk. Reinsert the test diskettes when prompted.

5. When the message box informs you that testing is complete, select OK to close the box.

6. Click on the Backup button to return to the Backup window.

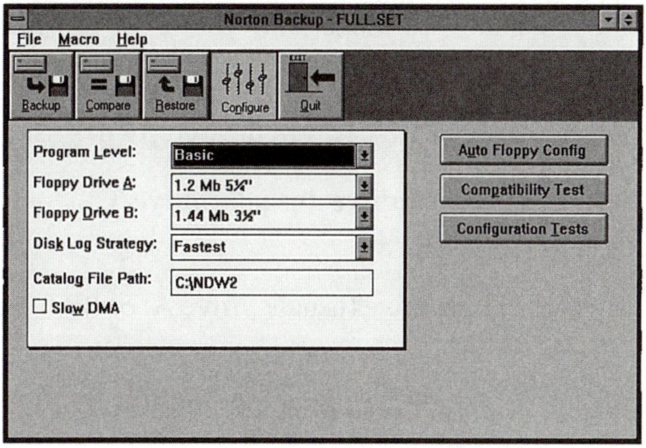

Figure 12.2 The Configure window.

When configuration is complete, you must select a user level for the program. Most users should select the default Basic level. Follow these steps to set your user level:

1. From the main Norton Backup screen, click on the Configure button.

2. When the Configure window appears, select the Basic option from the Program Level list.

3. Click on the Backup button to return to the Backup window.

Starting the Backup Process

There are numerous options you can select for backing up your data; this book discusses only those options needed for a normal backup. To initiate a normal backup, follow these steps:

1. With Norton Backup for Windows running, click the Backup button to make sure you're in the Backup window.

2. Select DEFAULT.SET from the Setup Files list.

3. Select the source drive (usually drive C:) from the Backup From list.

4. Select the target drive (usually drive A: or B:) from the Backup To list.

5. Select Full from the Backup Type list.

6. Click on Start Backup to begin the backup.

7. Insert blank diskettes as prompted.

Back Up Selected Files

You can also specify files or directories to back up. Follow these steps:

1. From the main Norton Backup window, click on the Select Files button.

2. When the Select Backup Files window appears (as shown in Figure 12.3), double-click the left mouse button on those individual files or directories you want to back up. Selected files have a black box next to their names; double-clicking deselects these files.

3. Click on OK to return to the main Norton Backup window.

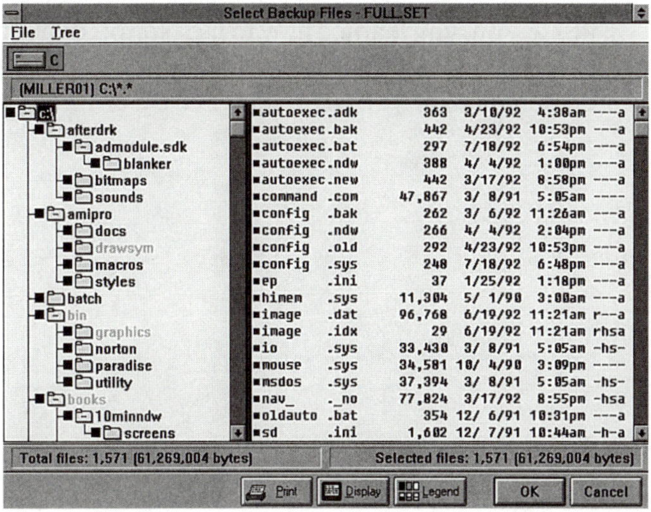

Figure 12.3 The Select Backup Files window.

Using Drag and Drop You can also back up small groups of files without launching Norton Backup. Just open a drive window, select the files, drag them from the drive window, and drop them on the Norton Backup icon. Norton Backup automatically launches and backs up the selected files.

Automating Backups

You can use another Norton Desktop tool, Scheduler, to automate your backup procedure. (Scheduler is discussed in Lesson 25.) A special Scheduler event called Automatic Backup is included with Norton Desktop. This event automatically schedules your system to launch a backup session at the same time every day. Make sure that you load Scheduler automatically so this event runs every day!

In this lesson, you learned how to use Norton Backup to protect your valuable data. In the next lesson, you learn how to restore that data to your hard disk in case of data loss.

Lesson 13

Restoring Backed-Up Files

In this lesson, you learn how to restore data to your hard disk from a set of backup diskettes.

If you have a disk disaster, chances are you can recover much of your valuable data—if you make backup copies on a regular basis. If you haven't made backup copies of your data, turn to Lesson 12 and follow the steps to create a backup set of diskettes with Norton Backup for Windows.

What to Do in an Emergency

There are two major types of emergencies you may encounter. The first type is where you lose only part of the data on your hard disk, perhaps due to an accidental erasure. When only part of your data is missing, you can use Norton Backup for Windows to restore your data.

If, however, your entire hard disk is trashed, you need to use the Emergency Restore Program on the Fix-It Disk that ships with Norton Desktop. This is a DOS-based program that can restore your entire disk—including the Norton Desktop and Norton Backup programs.

Using Norton Backup for Windows to Restore Data

If you can still start Norton Backup for Windows, you can and should use it to restore your data. Follow these steps to restore lost data:

1. Launch Norton Backup for Windows.
2. From the main Norton Backup window, select the Restore option.
3. From the Restore window (shown in Figure 13.1), select the proper backup files from the Backup Set Catalog list.
4. Click on the Select Files button to display the Select Restore Files window (shown in Figure 13.2).
5. Select the directories and files to restore and select OK.
6. Select the location to restore the files to from the Restore To list.
7. Click the Start Restore button to begin the restoration process.
8. When prompted, insert the proper backup diskettes.
9. When finished, Norton Backup displays an on-screen message. Click OK to end the restore process.

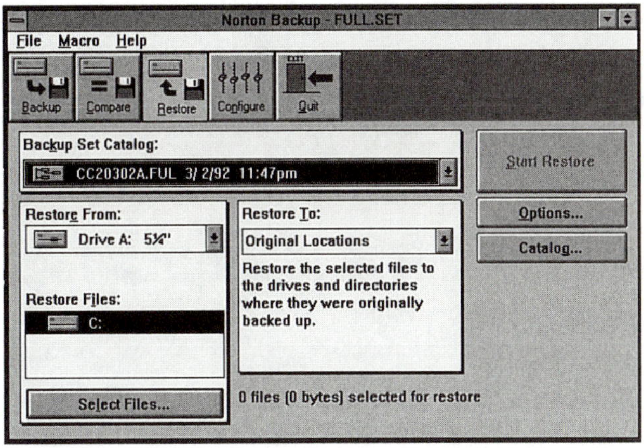

Figure 13.1 The Restore window.

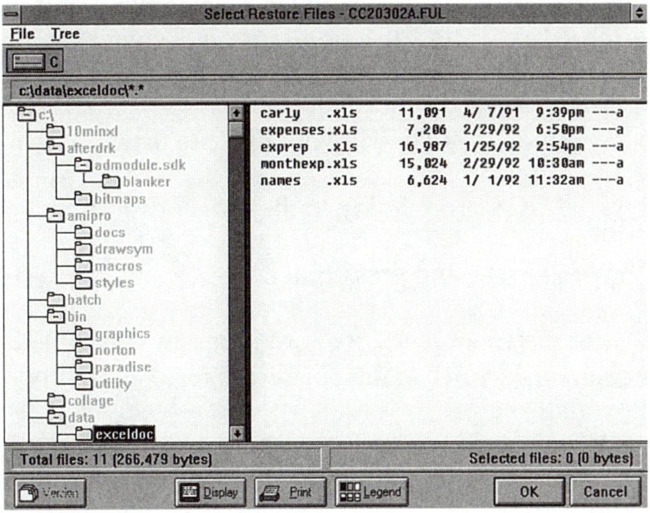

Figure 13.2 The Select Restore Files window.

Restoring Files to Their Original Locations You will almost always want to restore files to their original locations; select Original Locations from the Restore To list.

Using the Norton Fix-It Disk to Restore Data

If you cannot launch Norton Backup for Windows, you must use the Fix-It Disk to restore your files to your hard disk. The Fix-It Disk contains a special DOS-based Emergency Restore program that works with your regular backup files.

Before you can start the Emergency Restore program, you must first install the program onto your hard disk. Follow these steps:

1. Insert the Fix-It Disk in your diskette drive.
2. At the DOS prompt, log to the proper disk drive.
3. Type **INSTALL** and press Enter.

After the Emergency Restore program is installed on your hard disk, you can then begin the restoration process. Follow these steps:

1. At the DOS prompt, log to your hard disk drive (normally drive C:).
2. Type **CD\NRESTORE** and press Enter to change to the NRESTORE directory.

3. Type **NRESTORE** and press Enter to start the program.

4. From the main screen, choose the Configure option.

5. From the Configure screen, choose the desired options, and then select OK to return to the main screen.

6. From the main screen, choose the Restore option.

7. From the Catalog Options screen, select No Catalog.

8. From the Norton Restore screen, select the correct Backup Set Catalog.

9. Select the desired drive to Restore From.

10. Select Restore To Original Locations.

11. Select Start Restore.

12. Insert the proper diskettes, as prompted, until the process is complete.

In this lesson, you learned how to recover from a hard disk disaster. The next lesson shows you how to use Norton Desktop's SmartErase tool to undelete accidentally deleted files.

Lesson 14

Using SmartErase

In this lesson, you learn how to "unerase" files with Norton Desktop's SmartErase tool.

Have you ever erased a file by accident? With Norton Desktop's SmartErase tool, you can often "unerase" accidentally erased files.

Configuring SmartErase

SmartErase is installed when you first install Norton Desktop. It functions as a memory-resident utility that stores copies of recently erased files in a special directory called SMARTCAN. When you want to unerase an erased file, SmartErase restores the file from the copy in the SMARTCAN directory.

SmartErase Protects Non-Windows Files, Too Since SmartErase works as a memory-resident utility, it protects both Windows and non-Windows files from accidental erasure.

Since SmartErase can store only a limited number of files in the SMARTCAN directory, you must configure

SmartErase to make maximum use of its resources. You can direct SmartCan to protect all files or just certain types of files; you can also select how long to hold protected files and how much disk space to devote to the SMARTCAN directory.

To configure SmartErase, follow these steps:

1. Pull down the Configure menu.
2. Select the SmartErase option to display the Configure SmartErase dialog box, shown in Figure 14.1.
3. Make sure the Enable SmartErase Protection box is checked.
4. Select the desired options in the Files to Protect group.
5. Enter the desired data in the SmartErase Storage Limits area, or accept the default values.
6. Select OK to implement your configuration.

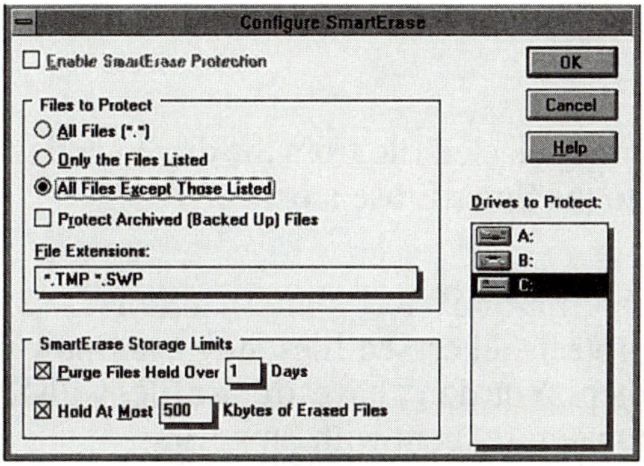

Figure 14.1 The Configure SmartErase dialog box.

Limit the Types of Files to Protect SmartErase can take up a lot of valuable disk space. To conserve disk space, you may wish to limit the types of files protected by SmartErase. For example, you may wish to exclude temporary (*.TMP) and backup (*.BAK) files from SmartErase protection.

Protect Your Files! If the Enable SmartErase protection box is dimmed, the SmartErase itself is not loaded into your system's memory. To load SmartErase to memory, add the following line to your AUTOEXEC.BAT file and then reboot your computer: `SMARTCAN/ON/SKIPHIGH`.

Erasing Files with SmartErase

If the SmartErase icon is visible on your Desktop, you can easily erase files using the SmartErase tool. Follow these steps:

1. With a drive window open, select the file you want to erase.

2. Drag the selected file from the drive window and drop it onto the SmartErase icon.

What about Regular Deletions? SmartErase protects all erased files, no matter how you delete them. You don't have to erase files with SmartErase to unerase them with SmartErase.

UnErasing Files with SmartErase

It's easy to unerase files with SmartErase. Follow these steps:

1. Double-click on the SmartErase icon or pull down the Tools menu and select the UnErase option to open the SmartErase drive window (shown in Figure 14.2).

2. Scroll through the directories and files until you find the file you wish to unerase.

3. Select the desired file then click the UnErase option.

4. If a question mark (?) appears as the first character of the file name, you will be prompted to insert the correct first character.

5. Click on OK to start the UnErase process.

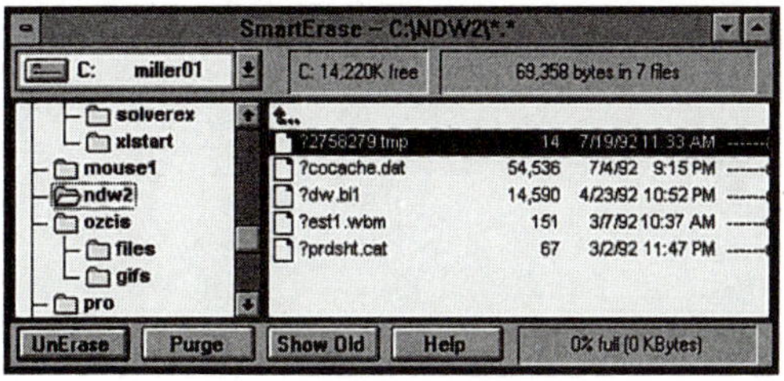

Figure 14.2 The SmartErase drive window.

Unerasing Old Files You will be unable to unerase a file if the file has been overwritten by newer data. (SmartErase will inform you if the selected file cannot be recovered.) For this reason, try to unerase files shortly after their accidental erasure.

Panic

In this lesson, you learned how to "unerase" accidently erased files. In the next lesson, you learn how to erase files so that they *can't* be recovered with SmartErase.

Lesson 15

Using Shredder

In this lesson, you learn how to erase sensitive files so they can't be recovered against your will.

When files are erased, the data in each file still exists on your disk until a new file overwrites that data. (This is how SmartErase can sometimes recover files that have been purged from the SMARTCAN directory.) If you have extremely sensitive data, however, you may wish to erase it in such a way that it *can't* be recovered. Norton Desktop's Shredder utility is ideal for this purpose.

Shredder works by overwriting an erased file with a special combination of characters. After Shredder has done its job, there is nothing left of the original file to recover.

Configuring Shredder

Shredder works well "out of the box" for most users. If you have special security needs, however, you may wish to customize Shredder's configuration. Follow these steps:

1. Pull down the Configure menu.

2. Select the Shredder option to display the Configure Shredder dialog box (shown in Figure 15.1).

3. If you want to delete data according to special U.S. Department of Defense security standards, check the U.S. Government Shredding option.

4. If you want to use a unique character pattern for overwriting data, check the Use Special Over-Write Pattern option and enter the overwrite pattern in the accompanying text box.

5. Specify the number of times you want the data overwritten in the Repeat Count box.

6. Select OK to confirm the configuration.

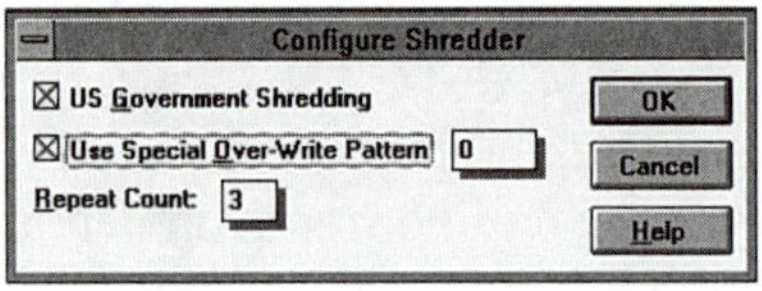

Figure 15.1 The Configure Shredder dialog box.

Shredding Sensitive Files

To shred confidential files, follow these steps:

1. With a drive window open, select the file you want to shred.

2. Drag the selected file from the drive window and drop it onto the Shredder icon.

Use the Menu System You can also shred files by pulling down the Tools menu and selecting the Shredder option.

You Can't Recover from Shredder Remember—when you use Shredder, your files are totally unrecoverable. Use this tool with caution!

In this lesson, you learned how to use the Shredder tool. In the next lesson, you learn how to view files with the Norton Viewer.

Lesson 16

Using Norton Viewer

In this lesson, you learn to use the Norton Viewer to view the contents of your files.

The Norton Viewer provides an easy-to-use way to view the contents of files without launching the associated applications. You can even look at multiple files at one time with special viewing options.

Launching Norton Viewer

To launch Norton Viewer, follow these steps:

1. Pull down the File menu.
2. Select the View option.
3. When the Open File dialog box appears, select the file(s) to view.

Launching Norton Viewer with Selected Files Open You can drag and drop to launch Norton Viewer with selected files already open. Open a drive window, select the files to view, drag them from the drive window, and drop them on the Norton Viewer icon. Norton Viewer launches with the selected files on-screen in their own individual windows.

Displaying Multiple Files

Norton Viewer can display one file at a time (as shown in Figure 16.1), or multiple files (as shown in Figure 16.2).

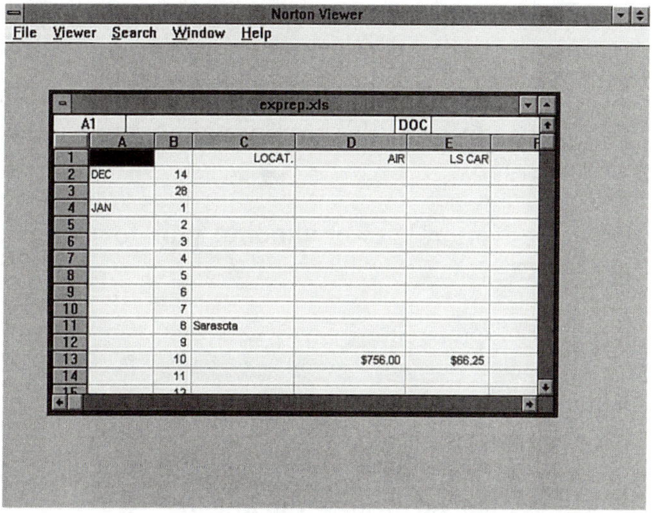

Figure 16.1 Norton Viewer with a single file loaded.

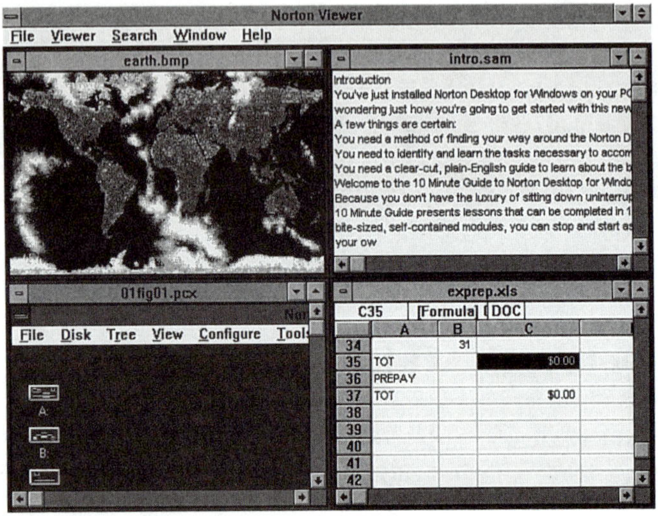

Figure 16.2 Norton Viewer with multiple files loaded.

To open additional files from within Norton Viewer, follow these steps:

1. From the Norton Viewer window, pull down the File menu.
2. Select the Open option.
3. When the Open File dialog box appears, select a new file for viewing.
4. Select OK to load the new file into the Norton Viewer.

You can display multiple files in several different ways. You can size and place the windows manually, or you can select *cascading* or *tiled* windows. To select viewing options, follow these steps:

1. From the Norton Viewer window, pull down the Window menu.

2. Select the desired option from the list presented.

Graphics Files Options

There are several options you can select when viewing graphics files. Among the options are:

- You can size an image to fit the current window by double-clicking anywhere in the image with the left mouse button.

- You can size the window to fit the size of the current image by clicking the image with the right mouse button.

- You can zoom in on a selected area of the image by drawing a box around the area with your mouse.

Text Files Options

There are also options you can select when viewing text files. Among the options are:

- You can search for specific text by pulling down the Search menu and selecting the Find option.

- You can go to specific cells in a spreadsheet by pulling down the Search menu and selecting the Goto option.
- You can go to specific fields in a database by pulling down the Search menu and selecting the Goto option.
- You can select different display fonts by pulling down the Norton Desktop Viewer menu and selecting the Font option.

Selecting Multiple Fonts You can select different fonts for different windows when viewing multiple files in multiple windows.

In this lesson, you learned how to view multiple files with the Norton Viewer. In the next lesson, you learn how to search for specific files with SuperFind.

Lesson 17

Using SuperFind

In this lesson, you learn how to use SuperFind to locate specific files.

SuperFind is a Norton Desktop utility that lets you search for files in various ways. You can search for files of a specific type, files containing specific text, files created during a specified time period, or files of a specific size. With SuperFind, it's easy to find the exact files you need.

Launching SuperFind

To launch SuperFind, follow these steps:

1. Pull down the File menu.
2. Select the Find option.

Initiating a SuperFind Search

While there are many options you can invoke with SuperFind, the basic SuperFind search process is simple. Follow these steps:

1. Launch SuperFind. The SuperFind window (shown in Figure 17.1) is displayed.
2. Select the types of files to search for in the Find Files list box.
3. Select where to search for the files in the Where list box.
4. Select any specific text to search for in the With Text box.
5. Click on the Find button to start the search.

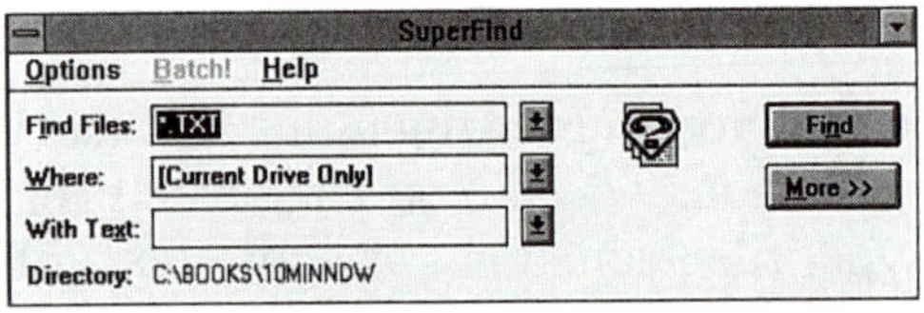

Figure 17.1 The standard SuperFind window.

When the search is completed, SuperFind displays a list of files that meet your search criteria, as shown in Figure 17.2.

Searching with File Sets

While you can type your own file criteria into the Find Files box, SuperFind comes with six predefined *file sets* you can use. A file set is a set of specific files to search for, as defined by file extensions. SuperFind comes with the following predefined file sets:

All Files Finds all files in the specified location.

All Files Except Programs Excludes files with .EXE, .COM, and .BAT extensions.

Database Files Searches for files with .DB? and .DTF extensions.

Documents Searches for files with .DOC, .TXT, and .WRI extensions.

Programs Searches for files with .EXE, .COM, and .BAT extensions.

Spreadsheet Files Searches for files with .WK?, .WQ?, and .XLS extensions.

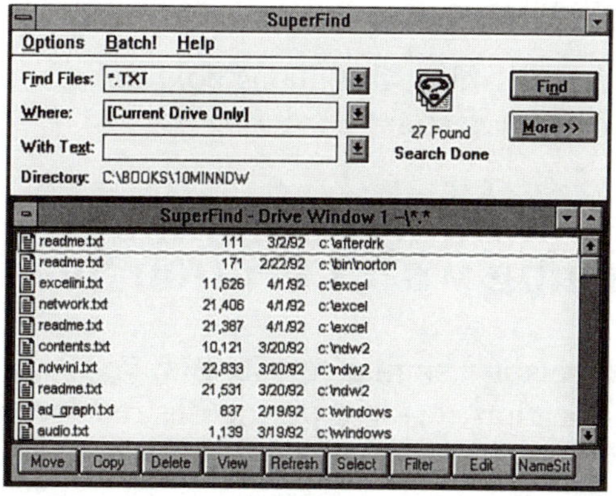

Figure 17.2 The list of files found by SuperFind.

To use a predefined file set, follow these steps:

1. With the SuperFind window open, click on the down-arrow button next to the Find Files list box.

2. When the full list is displayed, click on the desired file set.

You can also create new file sets. Follow these steps:

1. From the SuperFind menu, pull down the Options menu.

2. Select the Search Sets option.

3. When the Search Sets dialog box appears select the File Sets option and click on the Add button.

4. When the Add File Set dialog box appears, type a name for the file set in the Name box.

5. Enter the file extensions you wish to search for in the Definition box.

6. Select OK to close this dialog box, and select OK again to close the Search Sets dialog box.

Searching with Location Sets

Location sets are similar to file sets; you can use a predefined location set or type the desired location in the Where box. A location set specifies certain directories or drives for searching. SuperFind comes with nine predefined location sets:

All Drives Except Floppies Searches all hard and network drives.

All Drives Searches all drives on your system.

Current Dir and Subdirs Searches only in the current drive, directory, and subdirectory path.

Current Directory Only Searches only in the current main directory.

Current Drive Only Searches only the current drive.

Floppy Drives Only Searches all floppy diskette drives.

Local Hard Drives Only Searches only the hard disk drives on your system.

Network Drives Only Searches only those drives accessed via a network.

Path Searches only the directories specified in the PATH statement in your AUTOEXEC.BAT file.

Follow these steps to select a location set:

1. With the SuperFind window open, click on the down-arrow button next to the Where list box.

2. When the full list is displayed, click on the desired location set.

You can add new location sets the same way you add new file sets. Just follow the steps listed earlier, but select the Location Sets option in the Search Sets dialog box.

Additional Options

There are additional options you can select. To access these options, follow these steps:

1. From the SuperFind window, click on the More button.
2. When the SuperFind window is expanded (as shown in Figure 17.3), select Date, Time, Size, or Attributes.
3. Click on the Find button to begin the search.

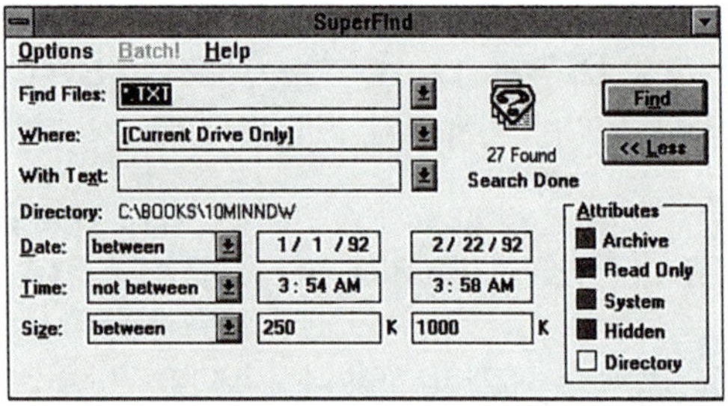

Figure 17.3 The expanded SuperFind window.

In this lesson, you learned how to use SuperFind to search for specific files. In the next lesson, you learn how to protect your system from computer viruses.

Lesson 18

Using Norton AntiVirus

In this lesson, you learn how to protect your system with the Norton AntiVirus utility.

A computer virus is similar to a biological virus, in that both invade your system, replicate themselves, and cause a lot of damage. Norton AntiVirus is a special utility included with Norton Desktop that detects nearly one thousand known viruses and eliminates them from your system, as well as inoculating your system against new and unknown viruses.

Computer Virus A *computer virus* is actually a computer program that copies itself onto other programs on your system. Viruses can infect either your executable program files (files with .EXE, .COM, and .SYS extensions) or your vital DOS system files. If left alone, viruses can destroy data on your disks and cause your system to crash.

Launching Norton AntiVirus

There are two parts to Norton AntiVirus. *Virus Intercept* is a memory-resident program that constantly monitors all files on your system for viruses. *Virus Clinic* is a Windows-based utility that you use to detect and eliminate viruses.

Virus Intercept is automatically loaded into memory when you first turn on your PC. It works in the background whenever your computer is running.

Running Virus Intercept Automatically If Virus Intercept does not load automatically when you start up your system, you need to add the following line to your CONFIG.SYS file: `DEVICE=C:\NDW\NAV_.SYS`. When you reboot your system again, Virus Intercept will automatically load into your system's memory.

Virus Clinic is accessible through its own icon or through the menu system. To launch Virus Clinic from the menu, follow these steps:

1. Pull down the Tools menu.
2. Select the Norton AntiVirus option.

When Virus Clinic is launched, the screen shown in Figure 18.1 appears.

Using Virus Intercept to Monitor against Viruses

Virus Intercept works in the background, never bothering you—*unless* it encounters a virus. If it finds an infected file, it displays an alert and stops whatever your computer was doing at the time.

If you receive a Virus Intercept alert, *stop whatever you're doing* and launch Virus Clinic. You can then use Virus Clinic to repair or delete the infected file.

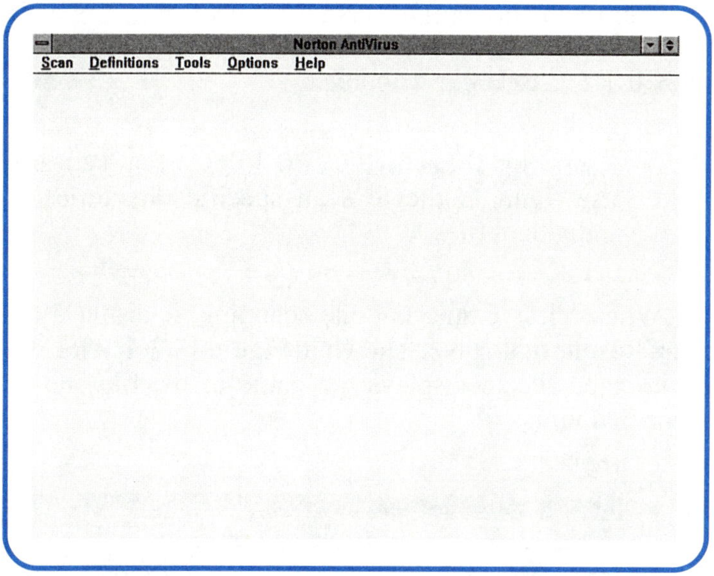

Figure 18.1 The main Virus Clinic screen.

Using Virus Clinic to Locate and Repair Virus Damage

Virus Clinic performs two functions: it scans your disk for viruses, and it repairs or deletes infected files.

When you first start Virus Clinic, it automatically initiates a scan of the drive you select. You can initiate a manual scan at any time by following these steps:

1. From the Virus Clinic window, pull down the Scan menu.

2. Select the Drive option to display the Scan Drives dialog box.

3. Choose the drive(s) to scan.

4. Click OK to begin scanning.

Scanning Directories and Files You can also use Virus Clinic to scan specific directories or individual files.

When Virus Clinic is done scanning, it displays the Scan Results dialog box, shown in Figure 18.2. If it locates an infected file, it displays the name of the file and its identified virus.

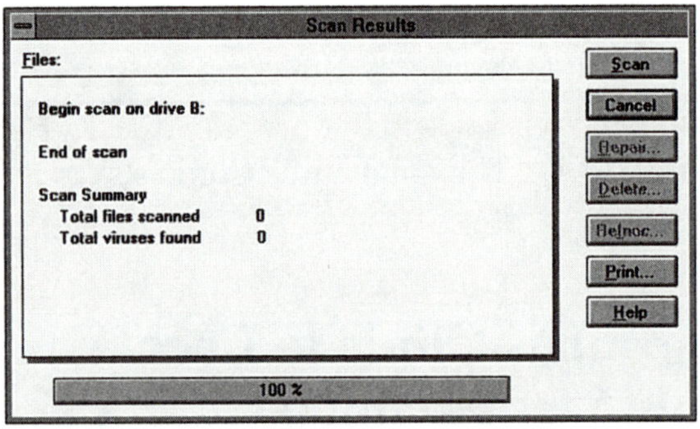

Figure 18.2 The Scan Results dialog box.

If you find an infected file, Virus Clinic can attempt to repair the file. Follow these steps:

1. From the Scan Results dialog box, click on the file you want to repair.

2. Click on the Repair button.

3. When the Repair Files dialog box appears, click on the Repair button to remove the virus from the file.

Non-Repairable Files If Virus Clinic cannot repair the file, the Repair button in the Repair Files dialog box will be unavailable.

If you can't repair a file, you must delete it. To delete a file with Virus Clinic, follow these steps:

1. From the Scan Results dialog box, click on the file to delete.

2. Click on the Delete button.

3. When the Delete Files dialog box appears, click on the Delete button to delete the file.

In this lesson, you learned how to protect your system against viruses, and how to use Norton AntiVirus to repair infected files. In the next lesson, you will learn how to make additional repairs to your disks with Norton Disk Doctor.

Lesson 19

Using Norton Disk Doctor

In this lesson, you learn how to use Norton Disk Doctor to perform preventive maintenance on your hard disk.

Disks can become damaged. They are subject to normal physical wear and tear, and sometimes contain flaws or develop defects. A damaged disk sometimes operates normally, but can deteriorate over time and threaten the integrity of your data.

Norton Disk Doctor for Windows is a utility included with Norton Desktop that performs six separate tests on your hard disk. If, in the course of performing the tests, it finds any potential disk damage, it alerts you. You can then use the DOS Disk Doctor on the Fix-It Disk to repair the damaged areas.

Norton Disk Doctor There are actually two Norton Disk Doctors shipped with Norton Desktop. The Windows version, discussed in the next section, is ideal for day-to-day checkups. The DOS version, included on the Fix-It Disk, is designed to perform major disk repairs.

Checking Your Hard Disk with Norton Disk Doctor for Windows

Norton Disk Doctor checks six different areas of your hard disk:

- Partition Table
- Boot Record
- File Allocation Table
- Directory Structure
- File Structure
- Lost Clusters

If it finds damage to any of these areas, it alerts you so you can repair the damage with the DOS version of Disk Doctor.

To run Norton Disk Doctor for Windows, follow these steps:

1. Pull down the Tools menu.
2. Select the Norton Disk Doctor option; the Norton Disk Doctor for Windows window, shown in Figure 19.1, appears.
3. Disk Doctor then performs some cursory system checks and then displays a dialog box listing all the drives on your system; select the drive you want to check and click OK.

4. Disk Doctor begins the major checks of your disk; if it finds a problem during checking, it displays a dialog box displaying the problem.

5. When Disk Doctor completes the entire checking process, it displays the Test Results dialog box; to display additional information, click on the Info button.

6. Disk Doctor then displays the Report dialog box shown in Figure 19.2; when you are finished viewing the results, click OK to return to the main Disk Doctor window.

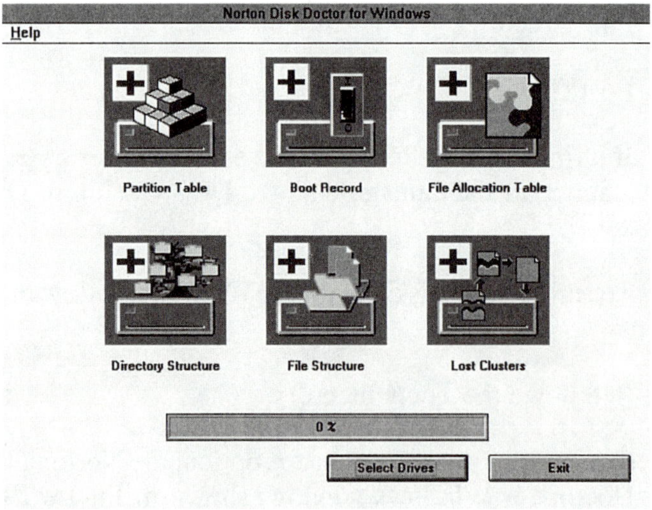

Figure 19.1 The Norton Disk Doctor for Windows window.

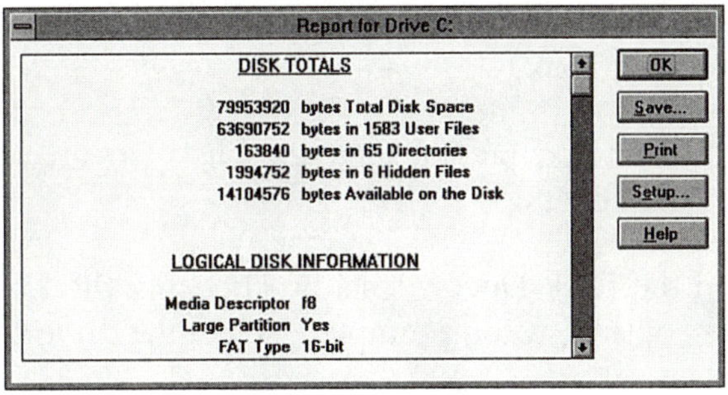

Figure 19.2 The Report dialog box.

If Errors Are Found If Disk Doctor for Windows identifies a problem, use the DOS version of Disk Doctor included on the Fix-It Disk *immediately!* If you wait too long to fix a problem, chances are you'll begin to lose valuable data.

Preventive Maintenance You should run Norton Disk Doctor on a regular basis, perhaps once a week, to discover any problems with your hard disk before they develop into something major.

Using the DOS Disk Doctor to Repair Damaged Disks

The DOS version of Disk Doctor is found on the Fix-It Disk. It includes the same tests as the Windows version, but adds the ability to repair damaged disk surfaces.

Follow these steps to use the DOS version of Norton Disk Doctor:

1. From the DOS prompt, change to the drive that contains the Fix-It Disk.

2. Type **NDD** and press Enter; the Disk Doctor opening screen appears.

3. Run the Disk Doctor tests by choosing the Diagnose Disk option; when prompted, select the drive to diagnose.

4. Click on the Diagnose button; Disk Doctor begins its analysis.

5. If errors are detected, follow the on-screen instructions.

6. When the Surface Test screen appears, select the desired options.

7. Click on the Begin Test button to start the disk surface analysis.

8. If errors are detected, follow the on-screen instructions to repair the damage.

9. When the tests are completed, the Summary screen appears; click on the Report button to see a more detailed analysis.

Panic

Some Technical Expertise Required Repairing damaged disks is a highly technical matter. Even though Norton Disk Doctor automates much of the process, you may feel more comfortable asking a more experienced user to guide you through this process.

In this lesson, you learned how to check your disks for possible damage and to repair that damage if necessary. In the next lesson, you will learn how to save your screen with the Sleeper screen saver.

Lesson 20

Using Sleeper

In this lesson, you learn how to protect your screen with the Sleeper screen saver.

An unattended computer monitor, constantly displaying the same static image, can incur permanent damage from *screen burn-in.* To prevent this sort of monitor damage—and to inject a little fun into your computing experience—Norton Desktop includes Sleeper, a built-in Windows screen saver.

Screen Burn-In Burn-in occurs when a ghost image of a static video image becomes permanently etched onto the phosphors that make up your monitor's screen.

Screen savers protect against burn-in by constantly changing the image on your screen when your computer is not being used. Sleeper includes numerous modules to display a variety of images while it saves your screen from damage.

Configuring Sleeper

You can configure Sleeper to save your screen after a predetermined period of inactivity. You can also configure each Sleeper module in various ways.

To launch and configure Sleeper, follow these steps:

1. Pull down the Tools menu.
2. Select the Screen Saver option; the main Sleeper window appears (as shown in Figure 20.1).
3. Select the module you want from the scrolling list at the left of the window.
4. Check the Hide When Iconized box so that the Sleeper icon doesn't take up valuable screen space.
5. Check the Load With Windows box to ensure that Sleeper is launched automatically when you start Windows.
6. Check the Enable box to ensure that Sleeper is activated.
7. Click the Minimize button to put Sleeper into action.

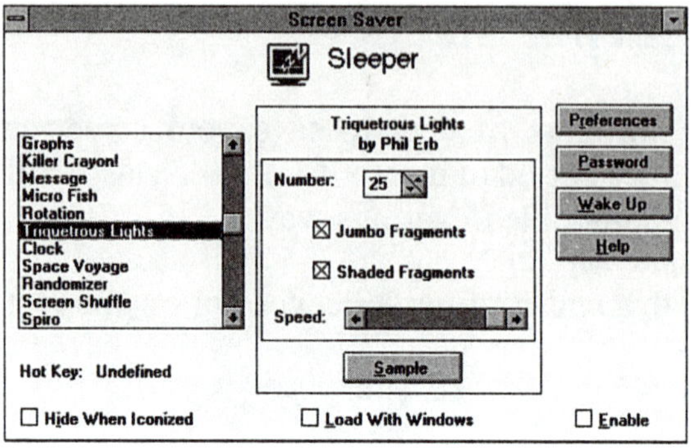

Figure 20.1 The Sleeper window.

There are other options you can select. If you click the Options button in the Sleeper window, you are presented with the Preferences dialog box (as shown in Figure 20.2). From this dialog box you can enter the amount of time before Sleeper activates, as well as corners of the screen that can activate Sleeper when you move the mouse pointer there.

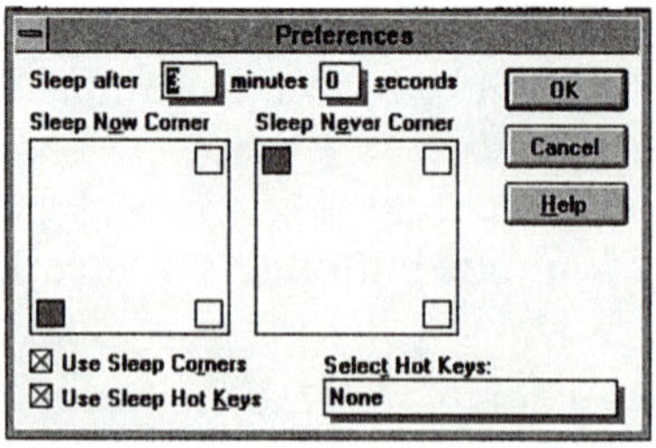

Figure 20.2 The Preferences dialog box.

When you select a Sleeper module, options for that module appear in the box in the middle of the Sleeper screen. To see the effects of each option, click on the Sample button.

The Sleeper Screen Saver Modules

Sleeper comes with a variety of screen saver modules. These include:

Animation Gallery Displays a series of animated line drawings.

Art Gallery Displays a series of nonanimated line drawings.

Bouncing Lines Example Displays one or two horizontal lines that bounce between the top and bottom of your screen.

Clock Displays a moving clock on-screen; the clock can be either digital or analog.

Fading Away Fades the screen to black, pixel by pixel.

Killer Crayon! An on-screen game that runs by itself when you're not around.

Message Displays a moving message of your choice on the screen.

Micro Fish Displays a computerized aquarium, complete with fish and air bubbles.

Rotation Displays a group of rotating wire-frame objects.

Screen Shuffle Cuts your screen into a series of squares, and then shuffles them around.

Space Voyage Displays a moving star field.

Spiro Displays random symmetrical line images, like the old SpiroGraph toy.

Spotlight Blacks out your screen and then displays a spotlight that highlights areas of your original screen.

Staring Eyes Displays moving sets of staring eyes.

Starless Night Displays a black screen.

Tornados Displays a series of whirling tornados.

Triquetrous Lights Displays an explosion that breaks into numerous fragments.

Trivia Displays a series of trivia questions.

In this lesson, you learned about Sleeper, Norton Desktop's built-in screen saver. In the next lesson, you'll learn about Norton Desktop's three built-in calculators.

Lesson 21

Using the Calculators

In this lesson, you learn about Norton Desktop's three built-in calculators.

Norton Desktop includes three built-in calculators. All operate similarly to regular hand-held or desktop calculators, and help you perform quick mathematical operations from within Norton Desktop.

The three calculators are:

- Tape Calculator
- Scientific Calculator
- Financial Calculator

Launching and Selecting a Calculator

To launch a calculator, follow these steps:

1. Pull down the Tools menu.
2. Select Calculator.

The last-used calculator appears on your Desktop. To change to a different calculator, follow these steps:

1. From the calculator itself, pull down the Calculator menu.

2. Select the desired calculator from the list.

Using the Tape Calculator

Norton Desktop's Tape Calculator, shown in Figure 21.1, works much like most regular tape calculators. You can perform simple operations by either clicking the on-screen buttons with the mouse or using the numeric keypad on your keyboard.

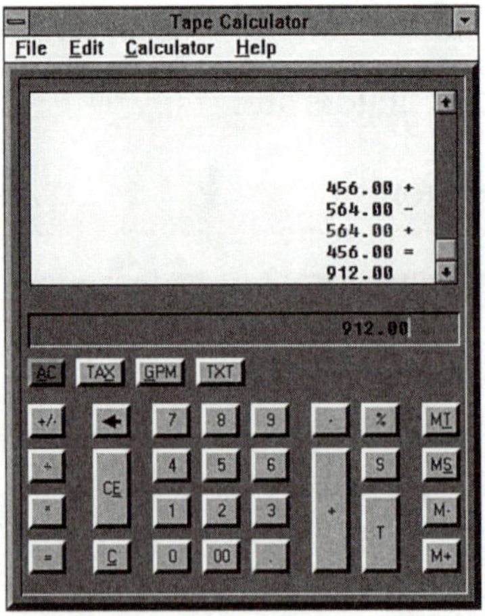

Figure 21.1 The Tape Calculator.

Input Order The Tape Calculator can accept normal input order or Reverse Polish Notation (RPN). Where normal input order is used by most hand-held calculators, RPN works more like an adding machine. To change input modes, pull down the calculator's File menu and select the Setup option. When the Setup dialog box appears, select either Infix for standard mode, or RPN for Reverse Polish Notation.

The Tape Calculator also includes a few extra functions. These include:

TAX Function Pressing this button lets you add sales tax to any item. (You must first set your state's sales tax in the Setup dialog box.)

GPM Function Pressing this button lets you calculate gross profits, if you know an item's cost and your gross profit margin.

TXT Mode Pressing this button activates the Text mode, which lets you annotate any data entry with text typed from the keyboard.

Tape Mode This mode emulates the tape in a normal tape calculator. You can save the tape by pulling down the File menu and selecting the Save Tape As option. To print a tape, pull down the File menu and select the Print Tape option.

Using the Scientific Calculator

Norton Desktop's Scientific Calculator, shown in Figure 21.2, includes most of the same functions you would find on a professional hand-held scientific calculator. It uses Reverse Polish Notation exclusively, and lets you perform dozens of scientific and technical operations.

Figure 21.2 The Scientific Calculator.

Using the Financial Calculator

Norton Desktop's Financial Calculator, shown in Figure 21.3, operates in the same fashion as the Scientific Calculator (using Reverse Polish Notation), but includes many useful financial functions. Many of the special functions are accessed by pulling down the calculator's Compute menu.

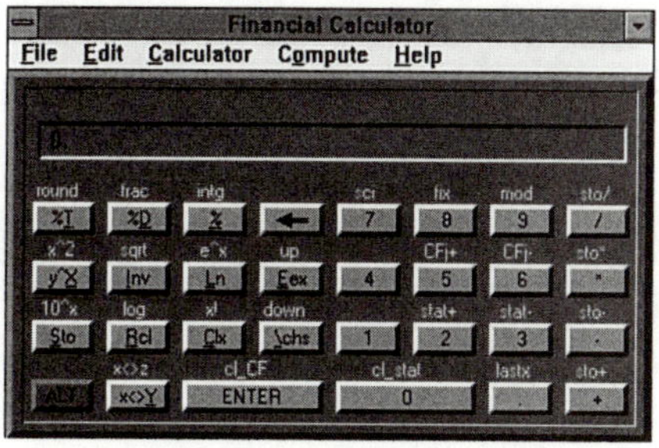

Figure 21.3 The Financial Calculator.

The special financial functions include:

Amortization Calculates the monthly payment and amortization of a loan, based on a specified interest rate and length of loan.

Bond Calculates bond prices, based on desired yield.

Date/Time Calculates the exact difference between two dates, for financial purposes.

Depreciation Calculates the depreciated value and accumulated value of any depreciable asset.

Discounted Cash Flow Calculates discounted cash flow, using either the net present value or the internal rate of return methods.

Simple Interest Calculates the accrued interest and total principle plus interest on a simple-interest loan.

Statistics Calculates average, standard deviation, weighted average, summation (total), summation of *x* (or *y*) squared, and summation of *x* times *y* for any set of *x* and *y* values.

In this lesson, you learned about Norton Desktop's three built-in calculators. In the next lesson, you'll learn how to use the Desktop Editor to edit your text files.

Lesson 22

Using Desktop Editor

In this lesson, you learn how to use Norton Desktop's Desktop Editor to edit text files.

The Desktop Editor is a Norton Desktop utility that lets you edit small text files. It works much like full-featured word processing programs, but is specially designed to work with ASCII text files, such as the AUTOEXEC.BAT and CONFIG.SYS files.

Launching Desktop Editor

To launch Desktop Editor, follow these steps:

1. Pull down the Tools menu.
2. Select the Desktop Editor option.

   The Desktop Editor window, as shown in Figure 22.1, appears.

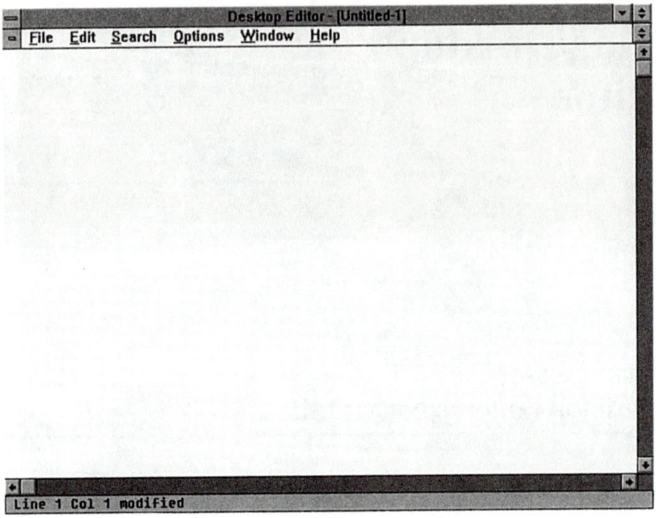

Figure 22.1 The Desktop Editor window.

Opening a File

To open an existing file, follow these steps:

1. Pull down the File menu.
2. Select the Open option.
3. When the Open File dialog box appears, select the desired file.
4. Click on OK to open the file.

To create a new file, follow these steps:

1. Pull down the File menu.

2. Select the New option.

Editing a File

Once a file is on-screen, you can move to any point in the text by moving the cursor with either the mouse or the arrow keys on your keyboard. You can cut, copy, and paste text from different areas in your document, or between multiple documents. To access editing functions, follow these steps:

1. Pull down the Edit window, as shown in Figure 22.2.

2. Select the desired edit function.

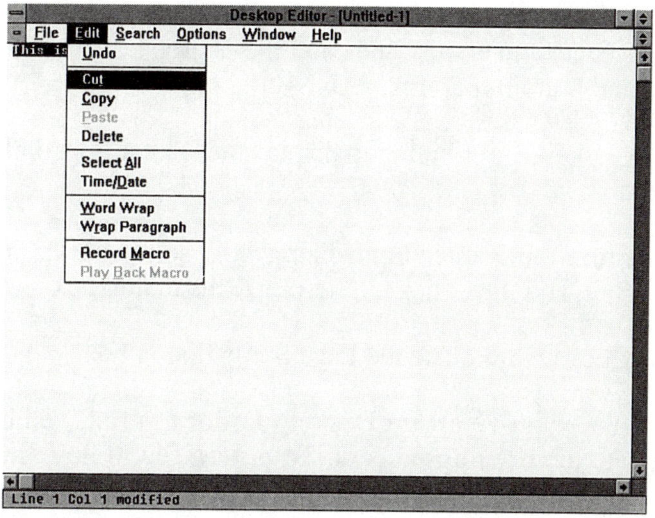

Figure 22.2 The Edit menu.

Printing a File

Before you can print a file, you must first select several options within Desktop Editor. To configure Desktop Editor for printing, follow these steps:

1. Pull down the File menu.

2. Select the Printer Setup option.

3. When the Printer Setup dialog box appears, select the desired printer; click OK to close this dialog box.

4. Pull down the File menu.

5. Select the Page Setup option.

6. When the Page Setup dialog box appears, edit the Header and Footer, and enter the desired left, right, top, and bottom margins.

7. Click the Font button to display the Printer Font dialog box.

8. From the Printer Font dialog box, select the desired font, and then click OK to close this dialog box.

9. Click OK to close the Page Setup dialog box.

After you've set up Desktop Editor to print, you can initiate the printing process. To print a file, follow these steps:

1. Pull down the File menu.

2. Select the Print option.

Saving and Closing a File

When you're done editing your file, you must save and then close the file.

To save a new file, follow these steps:

1. Pull down the File menu.
2. Select the Save As option.
3. When the Save As dialog box appears, type the new name for the document and click OK.

To save changes to an existing file, follow these steps:

1. Pull down the File menu.
2. Select the Save option.

To close a file, follow these steps:

1. Pull down the File menu.
2. Select the Close command.

Closing and Saving When you close an unsaved file, you will be prompted to save the file at that point.

In this lesson, you learned how to edit small text files with the Desktop Editor. In the next lesson, you'll learn how to edit desktop icons with the Icon Editor.

Lesson 23

Using Icon Editor

In this lesson, you learn how to create and edit desktop icons with Norton Desktop's Icon Editor.

There are hundreds of icons available with Windows, Windows applications, and Norton Desktop for Windows. With Icon Editor you can edit any of these icons, or create new icons to replace existing icons.

Icon Files Icons can be stored in various file formats. Stand-alone icon files have an .ICO extension. Groups of icons—called *icon libraries*—have .NIL extensions. Windows dynamic link libraries contain icons, and have .DLL extensions. In addition, normal Windows program files, with .EXE extensions, contain their own icons. Icon Editor can edit icons from any of these types of files.

Launching Icon Editor

To launch Icon Editor, follow these steps:

1. Pull down the Tools menu.
2. Select the Icon Editor option.

The Parts of the Icon Editor Window

The main elements of the Icon Editor window (see Figure 23.1) are:

Workspace Consists of a 32×32 grid that displays an enlarged view of the icon.

Tools Palette Contains the tools used to edit icons: Brush, Filler, Rectangle, Filled Rectangle, Circle, Filled Circle, Line, and Replacer.

Brush Size Palette Contains four different sizes of brushes for editing purposes.

Icon Display Displays the icon being edited at real size.

Color Assignment Box Assigns different colors to the left and the right mouse buttons.

Color Palette Contains all available colors for icon editing, plus `scr` to paint the color of the current background screen, and `inv` to paint the color of the inverse of the current background screen.

Library Control Buttons Load and unload icons from an icon library; includes Modify, Insert, Delete, and Replace buttons.

Icon Selector Displays all the icons in the current icon file.

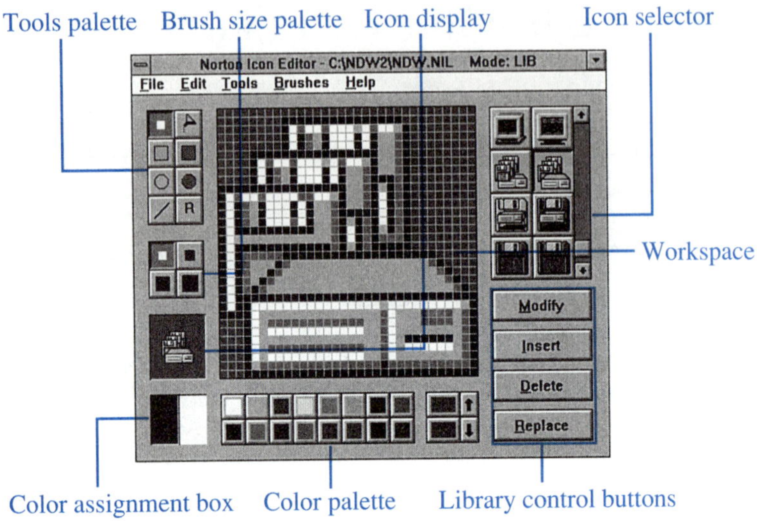

Figure 23.1 The Icon Editor window.

Loading Icon Files

Procedures for loading files differ slightly depending on the type of file loaded.

To load an existing .ICO file, follow these steps:

1. From the Icon Editor window, pull down the File menu.
2. Select the Open option.
3. When the Open dialog box appears, select Icon as the File Type.
4. Select the file you wish to load.
5. Select OK to load the file.

To create a new .ICO file, follow these steps:

1. From the Icon Editor window, pull down the File menu.
2. Select the New option.
3. When the New dialog box appears, check the Icon option.
4. Select OK to open the new file.

Icon Libraries To open an icon library file, follow the same steps as outlined for .ICO files, but select Library as the File Type in the Open dialog box. When you open an icon library, you must then select which of the icons in the library you wish to edit. Select an icon from the Icon Selector, and then click on the Modify button. The selected icon is now loaded into the workspace.

Editing Icons

To edit an icon you must use the tools in the tools palette, and assign them colors from the color palette. To select a tool, click on the appropriate tool button.

The tools in the tools palette are:

Brush Paints areas of the workspace either by clicking on individual pixels or by dragging the mouse across an area of pixels while holding down the mouse button; size is determined by the brush size palette.

Filler Fills an area with the selected color.

Rectangle Draws a rectangle in the workspace by clicking on one corner and dragging the pointer until the rectangle is the correct size.

Filled Rectangle Draws a rectangle with the inside filled with the right mouse button color.

Circle Draws an ellipse; works the same way as the rectangle tool.

Filled Circle Draws an ellipse with the inside filled with the right mouse button color.

Line Draws a line by clicking on one end of the line and dragging until the line is the correct length.

Replacer Works like the brush tool except that instead of painting an area with fresh color, it replaces the existing color with a new color.

To assign a color to the right mouse button, click the right mouse button on the desired color button. To assign a color to the left mouse button, click the left mouse button on the desired color button. You can draw with the tool using either the left or right mouse button in order to use the associated color. Figure 23.2 shows an icon editing session in process.

Watching Your Work Note that you work on the icon one pixel at a time. It's sometimes tedious work, but you can monitor your progress by observing the icon-in-progress in the icon display to the left of the Icon Editor window.

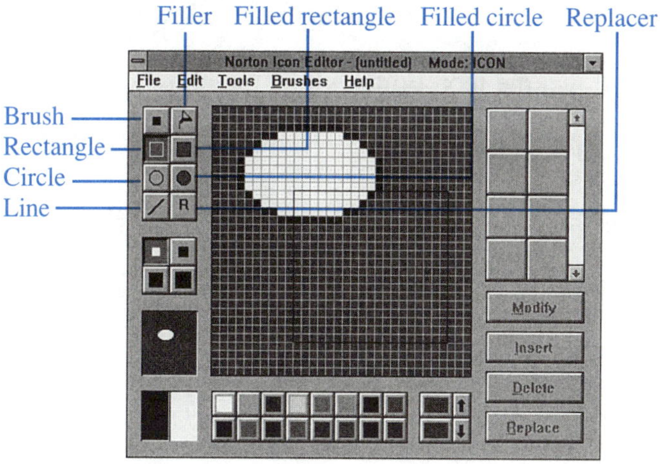

Figure 23.2 Editing an icon.

Saving Icon Files

When you're done editing your icon, you need to save the icon file.

Saving Individual Icons in an Icon Library

When you're finished editing an icon that is part of an icon library, you must return the icon to the library *before* you save the library. Click on the Replace button to replace the currently selected icon with the icon in the workspace, or click on the Insert button to insert the workspace icon as a new icon in the icon library.

To save changes to an existing file, follow these steps:

1. Pull down the Icon Editor's File menu.
2. Select the Save option.

To save the icon as a new file, follow these steps:

1. Pull down the Icon Editor's File menu.
2. Select the Save As command.
3. Enter the desired filename and select OK to save the new file.

This lesson provided an overview of Norton Desktop's Icon Editor utility. In the next lesson, you learn how to use the KeyFinder utility.

Lesson 24

Using KeyFinder

In this lesson, you learn how to use Norton Desktop's KeyFinder tool.

KeyFinder is a Norton Desktop tool that displays all the characters in a given font family. KeyFinder is especially useful when you need to use a special character—such as ®, ™, or ¢. You can identify the characters in KeyFinder and then cut and paste them into any Windows application.

Font Family A *font family* is a collection of letters, numbers, regular characters, and special characters with a consistent typeface. Each font family has a unique name, such as Helvetica, Arial, or Times Roman. *TrueType* fonts are special scaleable fonts built into Windows 3.1.

Launching KeyFinder

To launch KeyFinder, follow these steps:

1. Pull down the Tools menu.
2. Select the KeyFinder option.

The KeyFinder Window

The KeyFinder window (see Figure 24.1) contains the following elements:

Character table Displays all the characters in the selected font family.

Keystroke Information box Displays the selected character from the Character table and the keystroke combination used to create the character.

Sample Text box Lets you enter characters you want to cut and paste into other Windows applications.

Available Fonts list Displays all font families available on your system.

Font Sizes list Displays all available font sizes for the selected font family.

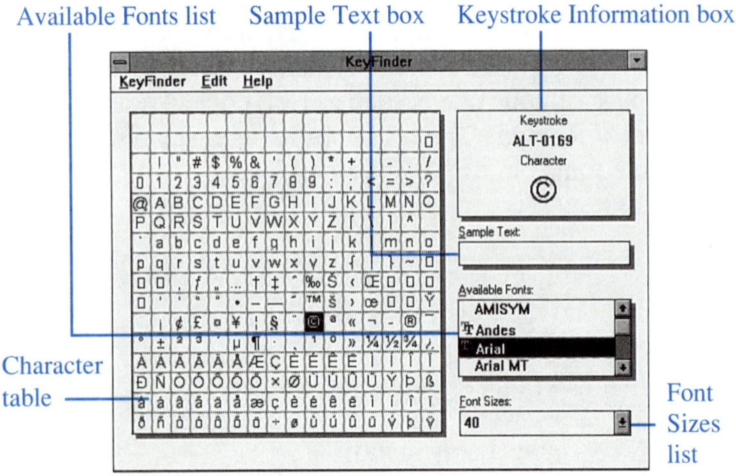

Figure 24.1 The KeyFinder window.

Inserting KeyFinder Characters in Your Windows Documents

One way to insert a special character into a document is to note the keystroke combination and use it to type the character into your document. For example, in the TimesNewRoman typeface, the keystroke combination for the © character is ALT+**0169**.

Use the Keypad When you use a keystroke combination to insert a special character, you must use the numeric keypad on your keyboard, and NumLock must be activated. The number keys at the top of the keyboard do not perform this function.

KeyFinder also lets you cut characters directly from KeyFinder and paste them into your Windows document.

To cut and paste KeyFinder characters, follow these steps:

1. Move from your Windows application to the Norton Desktop.

2. Launch KeyFinder.

3. Select the proper font from the Available Fonts list.

4. Locate the desired character in the Character table.

5. Double-click on the selected character to place a copy of the character in the Sample Text box.

6. Highlight the text in the Sample Text box.

7. Pull down KeyFinder's Edit menu.

8. Select the Copy command.

9. Return to your open document in your Windows application.

10. Place the cursor where you want to insert the character.

11. Pull down your application's Edit menu.

12. Select the Paste command.

This lesson showed you how to use KeyFinder to locate special characters. In the next lesson, you'll learn how to use Norton Desktop's Scheduler utility.

Lesson 25

Using Scheduler

In this lesson, you learn to use the Scheduler utility.

Scheduler is a Norton Desktop utility that functions just like an automatic timer. You schedule unique *events* into Scheduler's memory, which it then runs at the preassigned time. You can schedule both *program events*, which automatically run programs, and *message events*, which display on-screen messages.

Launching Scheduler

To launch Scheduler, follow these steps:

1. Pull down the Tools menu.
2. Select the Scheduler option to display the Scheduler window (shown in Figure 25.1).

Running Scheduler Automatically To make sure Scheduler is always loaded and ready to run, check the Load With Windows box in the Scheduler window. You can also check the Hide When Iconized box so that the Scheduler icon does not take up valuable screen space. If you elect to run the Daily Backup Event during Norton Desktop's installation, Scheduler is already set to load automatically when Windows is loaded!

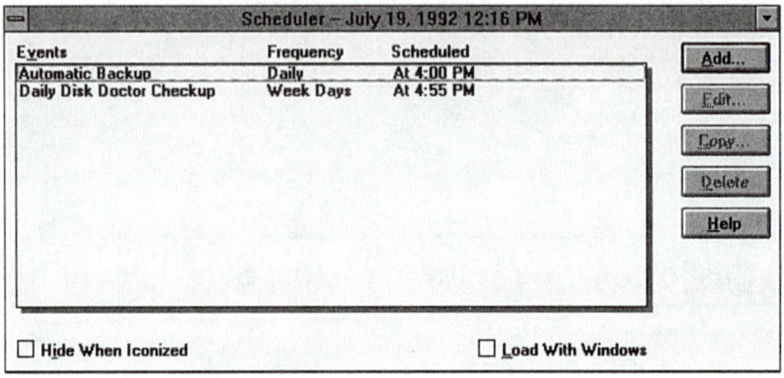

Figure 25.1 The Scheduler window.

Adding Program Events

To add a new program event, follow these steps:

1. Launch Scheduler.
2. Click the Add button in the Scheduler window to display the Add Event dialog box (shown in Figure 25.2).
3. Select the Run Program option in the Type of Action section.
4. Type a description of the event in the Description box.
5. Type the complete path and command line of the program to run in the Command Line to Run box.

6. Select the frequency to run this event from the **Frequency** list.

7. Use the Time buttons to choose the starting time.

8. If you choose the Weekly frequency, use the Day button to choose the desired day of the week.

9. If you choose the One Time or Monthly frequency, use the Date buttons to choose the specific date for the event.

10. If you Choose the One Time option, use the Month and Year buttons to choose the correct month and year for the event.

11. Choose OK to confirm the event.

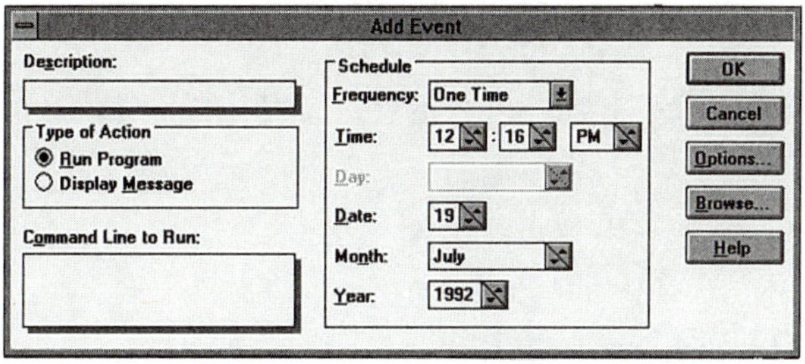

Figure 25.2 The Add Event dialog box.

When the proper time for the event arrives, your selected program will automatically launch.

Adding Message Events

Adding a message event is very similar to adding a program event. Select the Display Message option and type the message you want displayed in the Message to Display box. Then follow the remaining steps for adding a program event.

When the proper time for the event arrives, your custom message will be displayed in an Event Notification dialog box similar to that shown in Figure 25.3.

Figure 25.3 A sample Event Notification dialog box.

Editing Events

To edit a previously entered event, follow these steps:

1. Select the event to edit from the Events list box in the Scheduler window.
2. Click on the Edit button.

3. When the Edit Event dialog box appears, make your changes.

4. Choose OK to confirm your changes.

Deleting Events

To delete a scheduled event, follow these steps:

1. Select the event in the Events list box in the Scheduler window.

2. Click on the Delete button.

This lesson showed you how to schedule events with Norton Desktop's Scheduler. In the next lesson, you learn how to use System Information to display the vital statistics for your computer system.

Lesson 26

Using System Information

In this lesson you learn how to display the vital statistics for your system with System Information.

System Information is a utility that displays detailed reports about your computer system. You can use this information if you have problems with your hardware or software, if you need to upgrade your system, or if you want to fine-tune your system's performance.

Launching System Information

To launch System Information, follow these steps:

1. Pull down the Tools menu.
2. Select the System Info option.

The System Information window, shown in Figure 26.1, consists of a series of buttons along the top of the window. When you select a particular button, the report associated with that button appears on-screen.

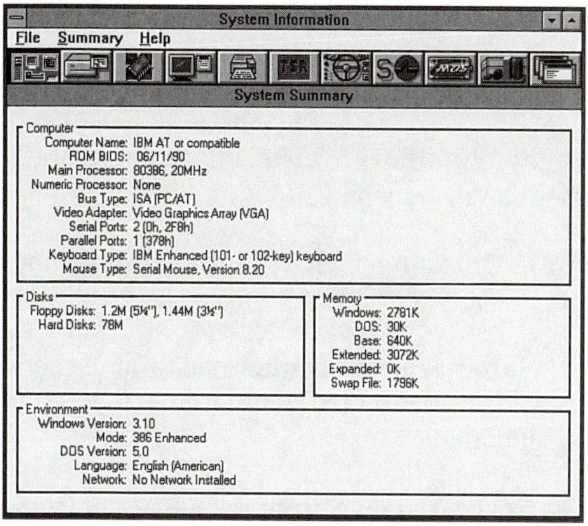

Figure 26.1 The System Information window with the System Summary report displayed.

Printing Reports To print any System Information report, pull down the File menu and select the Print Report option.

The System Information Reports

System Information provides eleven separate reports:

System Summary Lists basic information about the components of your computer system.

Disk Summary Lists basic information about the size and space available on each hard drive on your system.

Windows Memory Summary Displays the Windows memory used by fonts, device drivers, system libraries, and applications.

Display Summary Lists information about your system's video display.

Printer Summary Lists information about your system's active printer.

TSR Summary Lists information about terminate-and-stay-resident (TSR) programs loaded in your system's memory.

DOS Device Driver Summary Lists all DOS device drivers currently in your system's memory.

Software Interrupt Summary Lists the addresses of all software interrupts.

CMOS Summary Displays information about your system's battery-powered CMOS chip.

Processor Benchmark Tests Displays how the performance of your system compares to other popular computer systems.

Startup Files Listing Displays the contents of five important startup files: CONFIG.SYS, AUTOEXEC.BAT, WIN.INI, SYSTEM.INI, and NDW.INI.

Editing the Startup Files To edit any of the displayed startup files, click on the Edit command on the menu bar. This launches the Desktop Editor with the selected startup file loaded and ready for editing.

This lesson showed how to use the System Information utility. The next—and final—lesson explains how to use the DOS Fix-It Disk.

Lesson 27

Using the Fix-It Disk

In this lesson you learn when and how to use the DOS Fix-It Disk.

The Fix-It Disk included with Norton Desktop includes five DOS-based utilities that are invaluable in an emergency. You should keep the Fix-It Disk in a safe, accessible place in case you're ever confronted with an emergency that calls for the use of these tools.

The five utilities included on the Fix-It Disk are:

- Norton Disk Doctor
- Emergency Restore
- UnErase
- UnFormat
- Speed Disk

Norton Disk Doctor

The Disk Doctor on the Fix-It Disk is a DOS-based cousin of Norton Disk Doctor for Windows. In addition to analyzing your hard disk for defects, this version of Disk Doctor can also repair disk damage. See Lesson 19 for more information on using both the DOS and Windows versions of Disk Doctor.

Emergency Restore

Emergency Restore is a utility that lets you restore backup data to your hard disk in case of a hard disk emergency. You use Emergency Restore when you can't launch Norton Backup for Windows. See Lesson 13 for more information on restoring files with Emergency Restore.

UnErase

The DOS-based UnErase, like the Windows-based SmartErase, is a utility designed to recover files that have been accidentally erased. UnErase goes beyond SmartErase, however, in its ability to unerase files. It is more technically advanced than SmartErase, and therefore more difficult to use. UnErase should only be used as a last resort when you need to recover erased data.

To run UnErase, follow these steps:

1. From the DOS prompt, change to the floppy disk drive containing the Fix-It Disk.
2. At the DOS prompt, type **UNERASE** and press Enter.
3. When the main UnErase screen appears, select the file you want to unerase.
4. Choose the UnErase option.

5. Fill in the missing first character of the file name, if required.

6. Initiate the unerase procedure.

Manually Recovering Deleted Files If the automatic UnErase doesn't recover your file, you can choose to unerase the data manually. When you pull down the File menu and select the Manual UnErase option, the Manual UnErase window appears. Then you select the Add Clusters option and add individual data clusters until you complete the restoration of the erased file.

UnFormat

UnFormat lets you recover an entire hard disk that has been accidentally reformatted or damaged. Like UnErase, UnFormatting is a highly technical process that may intimidate some users.

To unformat a hard disk, follow these steps:

1. From the DOS prompt, change to the floppy disk drive containing the Fix-It Disk.

2. At the DOS prompt, type **UNFORMAT** and press Enter.

3. A series of dialog boxes appear, asking you questions about your system and your intentions. Answer Yes to all of them to proceed.

4. When you are given the option of performing a full or partial restoration, select Full.

As UnFormat begins the recovery process, a progress map will be displayed. After several minutes a message will inform you that the recovery is complete.

Run Norton Disk Doctor Immediately following an unformat procedure, run the DOS version of Norton Disk Doctor to ensure against additional damage to your hard disk.

Speed Disk

Speed Disk is a DOS-based utility that optimizes the performance of your hard disk. It does this by rewriting the data on your disk so that the data is in the most efficient order possible.

To run Speed Disk, follow these steps:

1. From the DOS prompt, change to the floppy disk drive containing the Fix-It Disk.

2. At the DOS prompt, type **SPEEDISK** and press Enter.

3. When Speed Disk loads, it tests your system memory and then displays a dialog box asking which drive you want to optimize; select the desired drive.

4. Speed Disk now displays the Recommendation dialog box. Accept Speed Disk's recommendation by selecting the Optimize option.

As Speed Disk proceeds with its optimization, it displays visual representation of your hard disk. This disk map, shown in Figure 27.1, shows you where all the data is on your hard disk. The more fragmented the data on the map, the slower the performance of the disk. After optimization the disk will be defragmented for optimum speed.

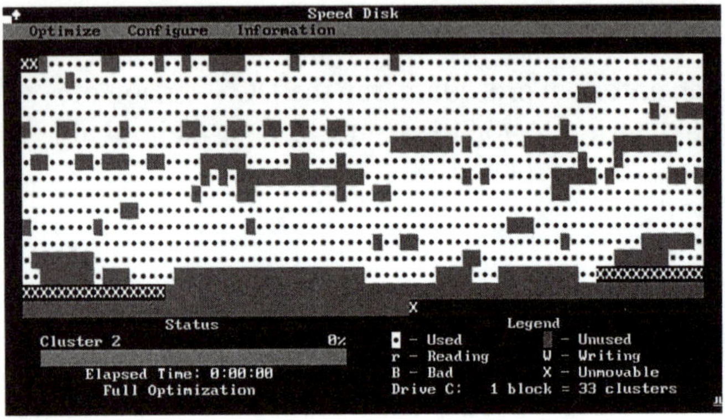

Figure 27.1 The Speed Disk disk map.

Other Options There are numerous other options available for running Speed Disk. Access these options from the Optimize and Configure menus.

This lesson showed you how to use the utilities on the Fix-It Disk, and concludes the *10 Minute Guide to Norton Desktop for Windows*. Remember, even though you've finished this book, keep it nearby. These lessons are also useful as reminders when you can't recall how to perform specific tasks!

Overtime

Appendix A

DOS and Windows Primer

This section highlights some of the DOS and Windows procedures you will use during your work with this program.

DOS is your computer's Disk Operating System. It functions as a go-between program that lets the various components of your computer system talk with one another. Whenever you type anything using your keyboard, whenever you save data on a disk, whenever you print a file, DOS interprets the commands and coordinates the task.

Windows is an operating environment that works with DOS. Windows sits on top of DOS and provides a user-friendly interface to some of DOS's more complicated procedures. Just as DOS functions as a go-between for the components of your computer system, Windows functions as a go-between for you and DOS.

The following pages explain how to run some essential DOS functions on your computer, as well as how to use Windows to perform more advanced tasks.

Using DOS

If you are running Windows, your computer has a hard disk. DOS is probably already installed on your hard disk, which means that when you turn on your computer, DOS automatically loads itself without any special installation. (Some computer manufacturers configure their computers so that Windows also automatically loads when you turn on your PC. If this is the case, you might want to skip to the next section.)

Once DOS is loaded, you should see a prompt (known as the DOS prompt) on your screen that looks like `C:` or `C:>`. This prompt tells you which disk is currently active; most hard disks are labelled as drive C. The diskette drives located on the front of your computer are labelled drives A and B. If you have only one diskette drive, it's the A drive. If you have two diskette drives, the top or left drive is usually A, and the bottom or right drive is usually B.

You can change to a different drive at any time by following these steps:

1. If you're changing to a diskette drive, make sure that there is a formatted disk in that drive.

2. Type the letter of the drive you wish to change to, followed by a colon. For example, type **`A:`**.

3. Press Enter. The DOS prompt changes to show that the drive you selected is now the active drive.

Managing Directories and Files in DOS

Because hard disks hold much more information than diskettes, hard disks are often divided into smaller parts, called *directories*. Each directory is like a branch off the main tree trunk; in the computer world the main tree trunk is called the *root directory*. Each directory branching from the root directory can branch out to other *subdirectories*; each subdirectory can also have branching subdirectories, and so on. Note that each directory and subdirectory has a unique name that allows you to access that directory from DOS or Windows.

Making Directories in DOS

To create a new directory, use the DOS Make Directory command. This command is invoked when you type MD, followed by the name of the new directory (including the complete path). For example, to create a directory called New, you would type `MD C:\NEW`.

If you wanted to create a subdirectory called NEW-A as a branch from the NEW directory, you would type `MD C:\NEW\NEW-A`.

Changing Directories in DOS

To change to a different directory, use the Change Directory command. This command is invoked when you type `CD`, followed by a backslash (\) and the name of the directory you wish to change to. For example, to move to the NEW directory, you would type `CD \NEW`.

If you wanted to move to the NEW-A subdirectory, you should type `CD \NEW\NEW-A` in the Change Directory command.

Listing Files with DOS

To display files within a directory, use the DOS Directory command. Follow these steps:

1. Type `CD` and change to the directory.

2. Type `DIR`.

3. Press Enter.

   DOS displays a list of files in this directory.

Copying Files with DOS

The DOS Copy command copies the selected file to a second location, either on your hard disk or on diskette. Follow these steps to copy a file:

1. Use the CD command to move to the directory that contains the source file.

2. Type the command line`COPY` ***`filename1 filename2`***.

   where *filename1* is your original file and *filename2* is the new file. You can also specify a new path for the target file, using the syntax *[drive]:\path\filename2*.

3. Press Enter.

   DOS then copies the file.

Deleting Files with DOS

DOS uses the Erase command to delete files from your disks. To delete a file, follow these steps:

1. Use the CD command to move to the directory.

2. Type the command line `ERASE` ***filename***.

3. Press Enter.

   DOS then deletes the file.

Using DISKCOPY to Make Backups of the 1-2-3 for Windows Program Disks

Before you install 1-2-3 for Windows on your hard disk, you should make *backup copies* of the original program disks. By using these backup copies to install the program, you avoid the risk of damaging the original disks.

Obtain several blank 5 ¼-inch or 3 ½-inch disks. You'll need the same number and type of disks as the disks from your 1-2-3 for Windows package. The type of disk should be marked on the package. There's no need to format the disks because the DISKCOPY command will do this automatically, if necessary. DISKCOPY differs from the normal COPY command in that it copies the contents of an entire disk. Follow these steps:

1. Change to drive C by typing `C:` and pressing Enter.

2. If the DISKCOPY program file is in a separate directory, change to that directory by typing `cd \(name of directory)`. For example, if the file is in the C:\DOS directory, type `CD \DOS` at the `C:` prompt, and press Enter.

3. Type `DISKCOPY A: A:` or `DISKCOPY B: B:`, depending on which drive you're using to make the copies, then press Enter. A message appears, telling you to insert the source diskette into the diskette drive.

4. Insert the original 1-2-3 for Windows disk you want to copy (the *source diskette*) into drive A (or B) and press Enter. DOS copies the disk into memory, then displays an on-screen message telling you to insert the *target diskette* (one of your blank disks) into the diskette drive.

5. Remove the source diskette, insert one of your blank diskettes into the drive, and press Enter. DOS copies the files from memory onto the blank disk, formatting it if necessary. DISKCOPY may prompt you to swap the target and source disk one or more times.

6. When the copying is complete, a message appears asking if you want to copy another diskette. Remove the target disk from the drive and label it with the same title and number that appears on the original source disk.

7. If you have another diskette to copy, press Y and return to step 4. Repeat this procedure for all the original 1-2-3 for Windows diskettes; remember to label each target diskette to match the corresponding source diskette.

8. When you have finished copying the last disk, answer `N` when DOS asks if you want to copy another disk.

Remember to put the original disks back into their box and to store them in a safe place.

Basic Windows Procedures

Windows is a Graphical User Interface (GUI) for DOS-based computers. Many users consider the Windows screen (interface) friendlier than the DOS prompt. Windows includes a program called the File Manager that allows you to work with disks, directories, and files. To properly use Windows, however, you have to master some techniques that might be unfamiliar to a typical DOS user.

Starting Windows

To start Windows, follow these steps:

1. Change to the drive that contains your Windows files, usually drive C.

2. Change to the directory that contains your Windows files, usually C:\WINDOWS, by typing `CD \WINDOWS`.

3. Type `WIN` and press Enter. Windows will start and display its opening screen, the Program Manager.

Using the Mouse

One Windows procedure that might be new to a DOS user is the use of the mouse. Mastering the mouse is essential to effective Windows performance. Here are the basic mouse procedures you need to know:

Action	Result
Point	Move the mouse pointer to an item on screen.
Click	Press and release the left mouse button once (quickly); often used to highlight an item in Windows.
Double-click	Press and release the left mouse button twice (quickly); often used to select an item in Windows.
Drag	Press the mouse button and hold it down while you move the mouse; this enables you to grab an on-screen object and move it across the screen.

While the mouse is recommended for most efficient Windows use, you can use the keyboard for many of the same operations. In many cases, Windows and Windows applications let you use special function key and combination key shortcuts to quickly access menu items and commands via the keyboard.

Managing Directories and Files with the Windows File Manager

Windows includes a special program called the File Manager. The File Manager simplifies many of the file-related tasks traditionally implemented by DOS commands, including working with directories, formatting disks, and listing, copying, and deleting files. Most users find it easier to work with the icons and menus of the Windows File

Manager than trying to remember the exact syntax needed to use traditional DOS commands. To open the File Manager, double-click on the File Manager icon in the Main program group.

Making Directories with the File Manager

The File Manager displays both a visual representation of your directory tree and a list of individual files in each directory. When the File Manager first starts, you are shown a tree with all the main directories branching off from the root directory of your current disk drive. You can change which drive is displayed by clicking on the appropriate drive icon.

To make a new directory, follow these steps:

1. Pull down the File menu.
2. Select the Create Directory option.
3. Type the path and name of the new directory in the dialog box.
4. Close the dialog box by clicking on the OK button or by pressing Enter.

Changing Directories with the File Manager

The File Manager displays a tree listing all directories branching off from the root directory. You can display subdirectories by clicking on any directory icon that shows a plus (+) sign. You can make any directory or subdirectory active by moving the mouse pointer to the directory name and clicking the mouse button. The active directory name is not highlighted.

Listing Files with the File Manager

To display the contents of any directory, follow these steps:

1. Highlight the appropriate directory or subdirectory.

2. Double-click on the directory icon.

Copying Files with the File Manager

Copying files from one directory to another or from one disk to another is easy with Windows. To copy a file, follow these steps:

1. Select the file to copy in the directory window by placing the mouse pointer over the file name and clicking the mouse button. The file name is now highlighted.

2. To copy the file to another directory, click and hold the left mouse button over the highlighted file, and then drag the file out of the directory window to the appropriate directory in the directory tree. (When you drag the file, the mouse pointer changes to a small file icon.)

3. With the mouse pointer positioned over the target directory, release the mouse button to drop the copy of the file into the directory.

You can also copy the file to another disk by dropping the file icon onto one of the drive icons at the top of the directory file window. Make sure that if the target drive is a floppy drive, it contains a formatted floppy disk.

Deleting Files with the File Manager

To delete a file with the File Manager, follow these steps:

1. Select the file to delete in the directory window.
2. Pull down the File menu.
3. Click on the Delete option.
4. When the dialog box appears, click on the Delete button to delete the highlighted file, or on the Cancel button to cancel the delete operation.

Appendix B

Ten Norton Desktop Tricks

1. Running Norton Desktop Tools from a Quick Access Group

It's often easier to launch Norton Desktop's tools from a Quick Access group than from the menu system. Just double-click the *right* mouse button anywhere on the desktop to display the main Quick Access Group. Then open the Norton Desktop Applications group, and launch the desired Norton Desktop tool or utility.

2. Changing Icons

You can change the icon art for any desktop or group icon. Select the icon, pull down the File menu, and select the Properties option. When the Properties dialog box is displayed, select the Icon option to display the Choose Icon dialog box. From here you can **B**rowse through other files and assign these icons to your selected icon. Two good sources for icons are the NDW.NIL file in the Norton Desktop directory, and the MORICONS.DLL file in the Microsoft Windows directory.

3. Making Your Own Menus

You can edit Norton Desktop's existing menu system, or even create your own custom menus. Just pull down the Configure menu and select the Edit Menu option. When the Edit Menus dialog box is displayed, you can add items to and remove them from existing menu system to create new, customized menus for Norton Desktop.

4. Recording Keystrokes as a Macro

Sometimes you can automate repetitive tasks by assigning multiple keystrokes to a macro. Norton Desktop includes the Macro Builder utility that lets you capture your Windows or Norton Desktop keystrokes. To record a macro, pull down the Tools menu and select the Macro Builder option. Macro Builder now records all your keystrokes until you click on the animated Macro Builder icon and choose the End Macro Builder option. You can then save your macro, and even assign it a keyboard shortcut key or assign it to Norton Desktop's Launch List.

5. Using Other Screen Savers with Sleeper

You can use screen saver modules from third-party screen savers, such as After Dark, Intermission, and the built-in Microsoft Windows screen saver. Sleeper automatically lists these modules in Sleeper's Image list box. Intermission modules are denoted by (IM) and Microsoft Windows modules are denoted by (MS). After Dark modules must be run through the After Dark Runner, listed separately in the Image list box.

6. Changing Display Views in Norton Viewer

There are numerous ways you can customize what you see in a Norton Viewer window. You can change the font used for text display in specific windows by pulling down the Viewer window and selecting the Font option. (You can use different fonts in different windows.) When viewing graphics files, you can size the image to fit the current window size by double-clicking on the image with the left mouse button. You can size the window to the full image size by clicking the image with the *right* mouse button. You can even zoom in on a specific area of the graphic image by using the mouse to draw a box around the selected area.

7. Comparing Two Documents with Desktop Editor

You can use the Desktop Editor to compare two different versions of the same document. Just pull down the File menu and select the Compare option. When the Compare dialog box appears, enter the names of the two files you wish to compare. When you begin the comparison, text is highlighted when Desktop Editor detects a difference between the two files.

8. Running the Windows Program Manager from Norton Desktop

You may wish to run the Windows Program Manager as a Windows application within Norton Desktop. (This is recommended when installing new Windows programs, which sometimes don't recognize Norton Desktop as the installed Windows shell.) To do this, pull down the File menu and select the Run option. When the Run dialog box appears, type **PROGMAN.EXE** in the Command Line box, and select OK. Program Manager launches, not as a shell, but as a normal Windows application.

9. Running the Windows File Manager from Norton Desktop

You may prefer to use the standard Windows File Manager instead of Norton Desktop's drive windows. To do this, pull down the File menu and select the Run option. When the Run dialog box appears, type **WINFILE.EXE** in the Command Line box, and select OK.

10. Uninstalling Norton Desktop

If you ever want to remove Norton Desktop from your system, you can do it easily. Open the Norton Desktop Accessories program group and launch the icon labelled Norton Desktop Uninstall. This special program lets you remove all or selected parts of Norton Desktop from your system.

Index

D

E

F

G

H

I

J-K

L

M

N

O

P

Q

R

S

T